50 truths

the devil doesn't
want you to know

Joseph Fielding McConkie

Ben Haven Books

50 truths

the devil doesn't want you to know

© 2013 Joseph Fielding McConkie
All rights reserved. No part of this book may be reproduced in any form or by any means without permission in writing from the publisher, Ben Haven Books.

For a complete library of this author's works, visit www.mcconkiebooks.com

Send all inquiries to info@mcconkiebooks.com

Printed in the U.S.A.

Contents

Introduction iii
1 Can God still speak? 1
2 What proof is there of Mormonism? 5
3 Who do we ask about God? 9
4 Why did Joseph Smith face opposition? 13
5 Why do so many attack the Church? 15
6 Who chooses our leaders and doctrines? 19
7 Would a loving God have only one true church? 23
8 Who can speak for God? 27
9 How does the keeping of records evidence
   that the Church is true? 31
10 Does God have favorites? 35
11 What's wrong with Bible religion? 37
12 What happened to the 12 Apostles? 41
13 What is the promise of the Word of Wisdom? 45
14 Does grace need works? 49
15 Why the law of witnesses? 53
16 Whose Church is it? 57
17 Was this work "done in a corner"? 61
18 How do we define resurrection? 65

19	What is the seedbed of all saving truths?	69
20	Can Christ's witnesses lack the Holy Ghost?	73
21	Does God have a body?	75
22	Who aided God in the creative act?	79
23	How can we tell what is of God?	83
24	Does agency excuse or empower?	87
25	Why is the knowledge of our premortal life important?	91
26	Is it God's doctrine to attack others?	95
27	What happens to those who never hear the gospel preached?	99
28	Can one be neutral in the cause of Christ?	103
29	Angels: Who are they?	107
30	What is a "living church"?	111
31	Is "inerrancy" inerrant?	113
32	Can common ground be sacred ground?	117
33	Do Mormons wear magic underwear?	121
34	Can true religion ask for less than our best?	125
35	Why does the cause of truth always attract scoundrels?	127
36	How many baptisms can there be?	131
37	Is tampering with the Bible alive and well?	135
38	Are Mormons secretive?	139
39	Who's in charge?	143
40	Eve: Temptress or prophetess?	147
41	Why is the Atonement central to all truth?	149
42	What is hell's favorite doctrine?	151
43	Do spiritual gifts exist today?	155
44	Does knowing require doing?	157
45	Are men and women equal in the Church?	161
46	Who can speak in the name of the Lord?	163
47	What is the plan of happiness?	165
48	Why did God create and people the earth?	169
49	What becomes of those who die as children?	173
50	The veil of stupidity!	177

Introduction

The need to worship is as essential to the soul of man as the necessity of breath to the mortal body. The atheist who claims no belief in God has simply chosen to worship at the shrine of his or her own intellect while the believer has chosen to worship that which is greater than himself or herself. It follows as the night follows the day that if there be a God in heaven he must have the power to save all that he has created and that he cannot and would not create that which was unworthy to be saved, for such an act would be beneath the station of a God.

By definition God is not and cannot be a tyrant. He did not create us to serve his every want and need, for he is not a slave to such things. He created us for the joy of creation: to share that same love that parents do in their own children. He wants us to enjoy all that he has and to be one with him in all things. Thus, at the time of their creation he endows each of his children with the gift of agency. In and through this gift we obtain the power to act for ourselves and are granted the freedom to do those things that will enable us to become as God is (Doctrine and Covenants 76:95).

Four principles must be operative for agency to exist. First, God, and he alone, must ordain sure and absolute laws by which we can advance and be blessed. Second, opposites must exist. There must be such a thing as right and wrong, good and evil. Third, we must have a knowledge of those laws so that we might conform to them or war against them. Fourth, we must possess an unfettered freedom to act upon those laws.

Again, it must be required of a God in whom his children are expected to believe and worship, to make the truths of salvation available to all to the extent that they desire them. This must be in such a plain and simple manner that no man, woman, or child can be left with uncertainty save it be of their own choosing.

In choosing the subjects upon which I have written I have in large measure simply picked those things I am most used to hearing the Church criticized for. It naturally follows that Satan insults and fights that which he finds most threatening. If something threatens him, that thing must be an evidence that the Church is true.

The fifty truths that constitute this work are a combination of subtle things; the significance of which often goes unnoticed. These are the kind of things that make the devil holler. The louder he hollers, the more threatened he is. These truths were simply the first things that came to mind. Fifty other truths would have served as well.

1
Can God still speak?

The First Vision is the foundational story of Mormonism. If it is true, Joseph Smith is the great prophet of the long-promised Restoration and it becomes the most momentous religious experience in earth's history since the resurrection of Christ more than two thousand years ago. If it is false, then Joseph Smith is but another false prophet separating himself from the many only by a more artful counterfeit than theirs.

The First Vision is the foundational story of the personal testimony of every member of The Church of Jesus Christ of Latter-day Saints. No true Latter-day Saint has claim to a testimony that is valid and binding independent of the witness of the Spirit of the truthfulness of this event and a faith in Joseph Smith's account of it.

There is no middle ground where the telling of this story is concerned. It will always invoke the spirit of peace, light, and truth, which in turn will always be countered by the loud, ugly ranting of the adversary.

If the story is true we know that the following are also true:

- God lives and interacts personally with his children. One must simply approach him with a pure heart and a faith unencumbered by the sophistry of men.
- Prayers are answered, and the heavens have been opened in modern times.
- God has not lost the power of speech, and revelation has not ceased.
- Ours is a living faith, not simply a history of a people who once had such a faith.
- All are invited to have their own sacred grove. This is not just Joseph Smith's story; it is a universal story. It is your story and my story. The scriptures are but the pattern, the experiences of the prophets the case studies. What God says unto one he says unto all (Doctrine and Covenants 82:5; 92:1). There is but one plan of salvation and it is the same for all of God's children.

To reject the story we must believe that a humble, uneducated farm boy living on the frontier of a fledging nation in the year 1820, was consumed with the desire to displace the historical Christian faith (along with all other systems of divine belief) with a message of his own making.

To reject the story is to set aside as myth scores of the most edifying truths ever vouchsafed to humankind with no better prospect than a return to what historians call the Dark Ages: to once again being governed by the creeds of men which have "filled the world with confusion, and [have] been growing stronger and stronger, and [are] now the very mainspring of all corruption, and the whole earth groans under the weight of [their] iniquity. It is an iron yoke, it is a strong band; they are the very handcuffs, and chains, and shackles, and fetters of hell" (Doctrine and Covenants 123:7–8).

One might say, "If the First Vision is not true, it certainly ought to be true. If God did not speak he should have. If he did not promise Joseph Smith, and through him, you and me, something better than the religions of the day offered, he should have. If ever there was a story that should be true, this is it."

What spirit, we are left to ask, would fight such a story? Our response can only be one that feeds upon the spiritual dependency and poverty of others. All else must say, "I too must pray about this, doing so in the hope that it is true."

The gate to Gethsemane for those of our dispensation is through the Sacred Grove. One cannot accept Christ while rejecting those who he commissioned to come in his name with his message. Any man or woman who does not have the courage to ask God about the truthfulness of the First Vision cannot have the truth. You cannot expect to drink the water from Jacob's well if you refuse to lower the bucket into the well. No man has a right to speak for God who does not believe that God speaks.

Truth 1
God's plan of mercy and justice must place all humankind on the same ground. The opportunity to receive it must be the same for everyone, for all can ask of God.

4

2
What proof is there of Mormonism?

As the foundational doctrine of the Restored gospel is the First Vision, so the foundational doctrinal of the meridian dispensation is the resurrection of Christ. If Jesus the Christ did indeed lay down his body in death and take it up again in life as an immortal and eternal being, then he must of necessity be the Son of God and the divinely appointed source of salvation for all men. The Book of Mormon stands as an independent witness of his resurrection, for it was the resurrected Christ that appeared to the nation of the Nephites to declare anew to them the covenant of salvation. As many of their number as could come forth did kneel down at his feet and worship him and bathe his feet in their tears. He in turn laid his hands upon their sick, lame, blind, and halt and healed them (3 Nephi 17:7, 9, 25). And in the process they became perfect witnesses of the reality of his tangible resurrected body.

The Book of Mormon is the perfect witness of the reality of the events attested to in the Old World and the best friend the Bible and the Christian message have. All professing Bible believers should rejoice in this new and independent witness of Christ.

The true testimony of Christ must also embrace the witness of the prophets he sent in his name. Thus the Book of Mormon testifies of the ministry of John the Baptist, of the writings of John the Revelator, of the miracles and teachings of Moses, of the teachings of Isaiah, and of the covenant God made with Abraham, Isaac, and Jacob, to name but a few. Again, in doing so it sustains the truthfulness of the Bible while bringing added light and truth to it. Nor is such a testimony limited to the prophets of old, for it is also the greatest witness of the prophetic ministry of the Prophet Joseph Smith and his role in bringing to pass the restoration of all things and the latter-day gathering of Israel (2 Nephi 3:12–14).

The Book of Mormon lays the theological foundation of Mormonism. Consider some of the great truths that we know simply because of this book. One is that angels still visit the earth to minister to men, women, and little children (Alma 32:23). Christ's commission to visit those of other folds will yet manifest itself as a great proof of the Book of Mormon (3 Nephi 15:13–18). The Book of Mormon is also the perfect evidence that the heavens are open and that much by way of marvelous revelation yet awaits us. As to the many doctrines taught within its covers, there are none that are not taught in greater measure and clarity than their biblical counterparts.

We have not taken as seriously as we ought the Lord's declaration that the Book of Mormon is the "foundation of my church" (Doctrine and Covenants 18:4). Doctrine and Covenants 20 is the revelation designated to announce the organization of the Church in this dispensation, to introduce the basic doctrines upon which it rests, and then to announce the restoration of the priesthood and the basic organization of the Church. Having announced the organization of the Church (Doctrine and Covenants 20:1-4) the revelation then makes a brief allusion to the First Vision (Doctrine and Covenants 20:5), and declares that the record which Moroni brought was translated by power from on high and attests that it contained "the fulness of the gospel of Jesus Christ" (Doctrine and Covenants 20:8–9).

The revelation states that the Book of Mormon is given to men to prove that the Bible is true, that the scriptures are true, and that God does and will call men to his holy work in this day and time as he did in ages past, thus proving to the world that he is "the same God yesterday, today, and forever" (Doctrine and Covenants 20:11–12). These events are then the great evidence that Joseph Smith was called to stand at the head of this the greatest of all gospel dispensations. To this declaration it adds that all who receive this record "in faith, and work righteousness, shall receive a crown of eternal life" while those who reject it do so "to their own condemnation" (Doctrine and Covenants 20:14–15).

The revelation then declares that "by these things," that is, the organization of the Church, the First Vision, and the coming forth of the Book of Mormon, we know that there is a God in heaven, and that all other principles of his gospel as taught in holy writ are true. This is to say that we as Latter-day Saints believe in God, the Eternal Father, and in his Son, Jesus Christ, and in the infinite Atonement worked out by him because of these events. It is to say that we have not built on the theological rubble of the past. We do not turn for our faith to the creeds of men, and we are not bound by the views of our Judeo-Christian culture. We stand independent of them all because every saving truth, every saving ordinance, and the authority to perform them has been restored anew. Ours is a new and living witness, not a new expression of old traditions.

A basic principle of law is that he who asserts must prove. That is, if you assert something to be true, you assume the burden of proof. If someone wants to assert that the Father and the Son did not appear to Joseph Smith in the First Vision it is for them to prove that the event never took place. Similarly, if we assert that Joseph Smith is a prophet and the Book of Mormon is true we assume the burden of truth. The Book of Mormon is the tangible evidence that these things are so. We anxiously share that evidence with those of every nation, kindred, tongue, and people. No other church on the face of the earth has such proof to offer.

Truth 2

No honest man or woman could read the Book of Mormon, stopping twice on each page to ask and answer the question, "Could Joseph Smith have written that?" and not come to the knowledge that it is true. The Book of Mormon is tangible evidence that Joseph Smith is a prophet and hence the Church he organized is God's.

3
Who do we ask about God?

The honor fell to James, son of Joseph and Mary and brother of our Lord and Savior Jesus Christ, to pen the single most important sentence ever written: "If any of you lack wisdom, let him ask of God, that giveth to all men liberally, and upbraideth not; and it shall be given him" (James 1:5). His expression is directed to the twelve tribes of Israel, who at the time of his writing were "scattered abroad" and whose words would actuate those events that would result in their being gathered again to the saving truths once known to their fathers.

"Never," said the youthful Joseph Smith as he sought to determine in what church the truths of salvation could be found, "did any passage of scripture come with more power to the heart of man than this did at this time to mine. It seemed to enter with great force into every feeling of my heart. I reflected on it again and again, knowing that if any person needed wisdom from God, I did; for how to act I did not know, and unless I could get more wisdom then I then had, I would never know; for the teachers of religion of the different sects understood the same passages of scripture so differently as to destroy all confidence in settling the question by an appeal to the Bible" (Joseph Smith—History 1:12).

Earth does not contain a more perfect description of the Spirit of Revelation than the one given in the verse just cited. Revelation is light, and light is the source of life. All true revelation has the power of life within it and thus is intended to perpetuate and give birth to additional revelation (Doctrine and Covenants 84:45). No revelation was intended to be complete and final. Such an idea stands contrary to the very nature and purpose of revelation; it is to argue that life was not intended to produce life.

Indeed, the greatest revelation of this dispensation was not the First Vision but rather the revelation that led Joseph Smith to the Sacred Grove where that great theophany took place.

How singularly interesting it is that The Church of Jesus Christ of Latter-day Saints has become the sole steward of the doctrine of James, that we ask of God. The challenge to ask of God is given by all Latter-day Saint missionaries to all investigators. No other church invites its investigators to accept James's injunction to so ask. Some demand that we acquiesce to the authority of the church. Others insist that answers can only come from reading the Bible; meaning reading the Bible as it has been interpreted by religious leaders, which excludes the thought of asking God, which thought they freely ridicule.

Has any priest or minister, when dealing with the knotty problem of Mormonism, ever suggested to their congregation that they pray about the First Vision or that they read the Book of Mormon and pray about it? All manner of effort is made to discredit both. Oceans of ink have been spilt, scriptural arguments are marshaled to the cause, history has been falsified, and witnesses perjured to that end. Would it not be simpler, more godlike, and more fitting for a church and pulpit to invite people to trust God by asking him?

From whence is the spirit that would have one man say to another, "Do not ask of God, for such is foolishness?" Recall the words of Nephi when he said, "For if ye would hearken unto the Spirit which teacheth a man to pray ye would know that ye must pray; for the evil spirit teacheth not a man to pray, but teacheth him that he must not pray" (2 Nephi 32:8).

In the Sermon on the Mount, the ordination sermon for the newly called Quorum of Twelve, Christ said, "Ask, and it shall be given you; seek, and ye shall find; knock, and it shall be opened unto you;

"For every one that asketh receiveth; and he that seeketh findeth; and to him that knocketh it shall be opened" (Matthew 7:7–8). As rendered in the new world this injunction is extended to the multitude, meaning by implication that the invitation is to all (3 Nephi 14:1, 7–8). The sacred truths thus sought were not and are not intended for the mocking gaze of the unbeliever or the ridicule of devils and others who choose to walk in darkness with them. They are as manna from heaven to those of the house of faith who alone are invited to feast upon their goodness.

To those of our day the Lord said: "But ye are commanded in all things to ask of God, who giveth liberally; and that which the Spirit testifies unto you even so I would that ye should do in all holiness of heart, walking uprightly before me, considering the end of your salvation, doing all things with prayer and thanksgiving, that ye may not be seduced by evil spirits, or doctrines of devils, or the commandments of men; for some are of men, and others of devils" (Doctrine and Covenants 46:7).

As every student of the Book of Mormon knows, Moroni concludes the book with the invitation to those who have read and pondered its pages to ask of God the Eternal Father if the things taught therein are not true. They are promised that if they ask with "a sincere heart, with real intent, having faith in Christ, he will manifest the truth of it unto you by the power of the Holy Ghost." The assurance is then given that "by the power of the Holy Ghost ye may know the truth of all things" (Moroni 10:4–5). This is not a promise to the reader that they will know all truth, that they will be able to give answer to all questions, or that they will no longer be required to walk by faith. It is the promise however, that they will have the power of discernment.

People choose their source to accord with what they want to hear. If you would like God to be the source of your religious faith you have the invitation to have him be such. For their own purposes people choose other sources. The honest truth seeker is duty bound to ask of God. Anything less than this is less than the truth.

Truth 3

All revelation, both institutional and personal, requires that we ask God. There is no gospel principle that can stand independent of this truth. Any church or minister that seeks to stand independent of this principle cannot be of God.

Why did Joseph Smith face opposition?

On the night of September 21, 1823, the angel Moroni, a resurrected being, appeared to Joseph Smith for the purpose of announcing the Prophet's place in the fulfillment of the words of the prophets of old and to acquaint him with events that would shortly come to pass. Joseph Smith said:

"He called me by name, and said unto me that he was a messenger sent from the presence of God to me, and that his name was Moroni; that God had a work for me to do; and that my name should be had for good and evil among all nations, kindreds, tongues, or that it should be both good and evil spoken of among all people" (Joseph Smith—History 1:33).

These words stand as a memorial to the Spirit of Prophecy itself. In ages yet future, they will be cited as the promised fulfillment of the words of all the holy prophets since the world began. Well might it be asked, "What is the probability that this unknown and uneducated farm boy, destined to eke out a living on the very edge of civilization will be known to both great and small throughout the length and breadth of the earth?" Further, the prophecy states his name will be known for both good and evil; that is, at its very mention there will be those who step forward to testify that he is the great prophet of the Restoration, while others will claim him to be an impostor and enemy to Christ. So it is with those called of God to hold the torch of light and truth. The brighter the light they hold, the louder the prince of darkness and his legions will holler. Of how many men in earth's history can it be said that their name was known "among all nations, kindreds, and tongues?" Such cannot yet be said of Christ himself.

There are none that will not be invited to hear. "For verily the voice of the Lord is unto all men, and there is none to escape; and there is no eye that shall not see, neither ear that shall not hear, neither heart that shall not be penetrated" (Doctrine and Covenants 1:2). No possible announcement could cause more wrath among any who have chosen darkness, self-indulgence, or ignorance over light. No speck of darkness stands unthreatened.

The best measure of a man is his enemies, not his friends. To obtain the praise of man, one must advance the cause of man.

Truth 4

Satan opposes all that is true. The greater the truth the greater the opposition.

5

Why do so many attack the Church?

Opposition, like wind against a ship's sail, is essential to the completion of the journey. If Satan ever ceases to lie about the Latter-day Saints it will be because they have ceased to be Latter-day Saints. One cannot march with his legions and not partake of his spirit.

It is philosophically impossible to reject the truth and not become a follower of false prophets. Among the most common signs of those who reject truth are that they will not ask of God. They will not humble themselves. They will not seek out their own Sacred Grove and ask of God. Another common sign that follows those of a resistive spirit is the freedom with which they choose the commandments they will and will not keep.

This spirit does not lead one to gather with the Saints but rather to withdraw from their company. It quickly reaches out to smother all that is good and to refuse the right to stand in the light to all within their power. Their darkness must be a shared darkness. In the true spirit of the adversary they seek all to share in their misery. Alma describes such a spirit in this manner:

"It is given unto many to know the mysteries of God; nevertheless they are laid under a strict command that they shall not impart only according to the portion of his word which he doth grant unto the children of men, according to the heed and diligence which they give unto him.

"And therefore, he that will harden his heart, the same receiveth the lesser portion of the word; and he that will not harden his heart, to him is given the greater portion of the word, until it is given unto him to know the mysteries of God until he know them in full.

"And they that will harden their hearts, to them is given the lesser portion of the word until they know nothing concerning his mysteries; and then they are taken captive by the devil, and led by his will down to destruction. Now this is what is meant by the chains of hell" (Alma 12:9–11).

Devils love to argue with each other. They find unity only in opposing the truth. Joseph Smith found that in telling the story of the First Vision, a previously divided Christianity "all united to persecute [him]" (Joseph Smith—History 1:22).

Often those who leave the Church do so under the guise of escaping oppression. The oppression to which reference is made generally reduces itself to someone magnifying their calling at the expense of someone else's time. What is of greater moment is that there are no gospel principles that can be rejected without at the same time rejecting the principle of agency. One cannot bask in the light without being consumed by that light and the desire to share it with others. Conversely, one cannot stand in darkness without seeking to repress light as it is found in others. As all things produce after their own kind so darkness is always the parent of opposition and persecution.

Missionaries quickly learn that when they commit someone to baptism all hell breaks loose. If we plan on going to the temple obstacles of every sort manifest themselves. The unexpected prompting to act is always followed by a recitation of the reasons why it should not be acted upon. Why?

When Satan opposes us we know that we are in the right place, at the right time, for the right reason.

> ## Truth 5
> Gospel truths will never go unopposed and the fight against them will never cease. Opposition is a sure sign of the true Church.

6

Who chooses our leaders and doctrines?

The Church was organized with six members on April 6, 1830. Joseph Smith and Oliver Cowdery were sustained to preside as the first and second elders (Doctrine and Covenants 20:1–3). Though they held the priesthood and its keys, they could not preside without a sustaining vote. The question is asked, "What if those who were to constitute its membership refused to sustain them?" The answer is they would have to go somewhere else and find a people that would.

"We have learned," wrote the Prophet Joseph Smith, "by sad experience that it is the nature and disposition of almost all men, as soon as they get a little authority, as they suppose, they will immediately begin to exercise unrighteous dominion" (Doctrine and Covenants 121:39).

The law by which the priesthood is governed precludes such behavior. The principle is stated thus:

"Behold, there are many called, but few are chosen. And why are they not chosen?

"Because their hearts are set so much upon the things of this world, and aspire to the honors of men, that they do not learn this one lesson—

"That the rights of the priesthood are inseparably connected with the powers of heaven, and that the powers of heaven cannot be controlled nor handled only upon the principles of righteousness.

"That they may be conferred upon us, it is true; but when we undertake to cover our sins, or to gratify our pride, our vain ambition, or to exercise control or dominion or compulsion upon the souls of the children of men, in any degree of unrighteousness, behold, the heavens withdraw themselves; the Spirit of the Lord is grieved; and when it is withdrawn, Amen to the priesthood or the authority of that man" (Doctrine and Covenants 121:34–37).

Further the Lord said, "No person is to be ordained to any office in this church, where there is a regularly organized branch of the same, without the vote of that church" (Doctrine and Covenants 20:65). As members of the Church, when other members are presented to us to serve as leaders, we are invited to raise our right hand in covenant to sustain them. In some instances pigeons may be called to preside over eagles. The issue is not who can fly the highest, or the fastest, or see the furthest; it is a matter of being able to fly in formation. We do not nominate those who will serve. The authority to do so rests with God. The right to do so rests with the body of the Church, for those so called need be "upheld by the confidence, faith, and prayer of the church" (Doctrine and Covenants 107:22).

The principles here described are the same as those that govern in marriage. The woman covenants to take her husband's name and to be one with him. The husband covenants to love, bless, and protect her. He can never ask of her that which God would not ask of him. The covenant to sustain and bless each other is always bound by the principle of righteousness, without which no covenant of the priesthood can be made or kept.

We have no doctrines that have the right to bully others doctrines. Our doctrines, like our leaders, labor in harmony side by side. Force or manipulation has no part of leadership nor can it be a part of any of our doctrines.

Truth 6

The Lord both created and governs the Church. Thus the leaders are of his choosing, as are its doctrines and ordinances.

7

Would a loving God have only one true Church?

As members of The Church of Jesus Christ of Latter-day Saints we hold to the doctrine that we are members of the "only true and living church on the face of the whole earth" (Doctrine and Covenants 1:30). If this is not the case Joseph and Hyrum Smith sealed their testimony in the Carthage Jail for no better reason than we have a wonderful choir, good youth programs, and the welfare system. These are not the things for which thousands upon thousands of people the world over gave up all they had to gather to Zion. These things are not the reason so many have been disowned by their families for joining the Church. They are not the reason we pay an honest tithe or respond to the call to serve whatever the cost in time or energy may be. Of the Old Testament Saints who died true to their faith and were gathered together in the spirit world to await Christ's advent there, we read:

"And there were gathered together in one place an innumerable company of spirits of the just, who had been faithful in the testimony of Jesus while they live in mortality;

"And who had offered sacrifice in the similitude of the great sacrifice of the Son of God, and had suffered tribulation in their Redeemer's name.

"All these had departed the mortal life, firm in the hope of a glorious resurrection, through the grace of God the Father and his Only Begotten Son, Jesus Christ" (Doctrine and Covenants 138:12–14).

Such has been the common lot of those who have held to the faith in all dispensations of time. Can we serve a God of truth in error and ignorance? Is it reasonable to suppose the time will come when those who seek after the truth will not draw the wrath of the prince of darkness? Why is it that God, who we are told does not care what we believe, becomes so concerned when the Latter-day Saints are involved?

In a discussion of religious issues few questions are more emotionally charged than that of whether there is only one true church. The announcement that only one church can be true, with its attendant implication that all others are false, gives immediate offense to many who suppose that such a conclusion excludes great hosts of wonderful people from the love of God and the blessings of heaven. It is thought to be incompatible with the idea of a loving God and often is labeled as intolerant and unchristian.

Thus we ask why such a question is so threatening. Does it not follow that if there are false teachers, false doctrines, false ordinances, false prophets, and even false Christs that there could be false churches? Is there not some significance in the fact that Christ did not affiliate himself with one of the various sects of the day? Is it not of importance that he organized but one Church, not a host of competing sects?

Surely no real blessings can accrue from falsehoods. To mistakenly swallow poison makes it no less harmful than to take it by design. Surely there are ideas that are as harmful to the soul as there are practices that are harmful to the mortal body.

If God is a God of truth, can he stand as the head of various churches that are false? Perhaps it ought to be asked, Is there law in the universe that governs all things? Must we discover and obey this law to obtain the desired results? If that be so, are there any fields that can be excepted from this principle, fields governed by chaos rather than law? Suppose, for instance, a dozen people add a column of figures and each arrives at a different sum—can all twelve be right? Suppose a dozen chemists set out to make a specified substance, and suppose also that they all attempt it by using different materials. How many of their number will succeed? Let us add another element and suppose that the people involved are very sincere. Can that in some way change things?

We need further ask, could the nature of our universe be such that law governs all save that which is spiritual? Could it be that in the realm of spiritual things chaos governs? Could it be that in some instances wickedness does bring happiness and in others it does not, and that there is no way for us to know what the result of our particular actions will be? If there are eternal laws, could it be that God has left it to each man, woman, and child to determine for himself or herself which of those laws will apply to each's situation and which will not? Is salvation simply a divine smorgasbord at which we all satisfy our own appetites, or would it be more true to all we know and have experienced to conclude that there are spiritual laws, just as there are temporal laws, and that "when we obtain any blessing from God, it is by obedience to that law upon which it is predicated" (Doctrine and Covenants 130:21)?

If such principles as righteousness, peace, and order are to be found in heaven then it must be a kingdom governed by laws. If there are such laws, then there must be a right and proper path that leads the soul back to the presence of the Father. All must follow the same path, just as all must follow the same laws to obtain results in the physical world of which we are a part.

Does the idea that there are spiritual laws that must be lived in order to receive the blessings of heaven make God unloving or unjust? Quite the opposite! The knowledge that there is a sure path and all are invited to travel it assures us of God's universal love and of his unfailing justice. A doctor cannot respond to the plea of his sick patient by saying, "Take whatever medicine you want. Whatever you choose to do will be just fine." Nor can we expect the God of heaven to respond to the distraught soul by saying, "Oh, any church will do; choose your own plan of salvation—whatever you do will bless you." If you are going to argue that the physician who knows what should be done for his patient but does not do it is without concern for those to whom he administers, you must also argue that a similar response from God would show lack of concern and love.

Singularly, it is in the doctrine that there is but one true church that we find the perfect manifestation of God's love and his justice. The notion that salvation can be found by following any path of one's choosing negates the need for a Savior, for obedience, or for righteousness. It does away with the need for faith and for religion in any organized form. It excuses us from any responsibility one for another and suggests that God does not care what happens to us. It further suggests that to be good parents we ought to let our children run wild. After all, to discipline them to a single standard, as the argument goes, would be unchristian. The Atonement of Christ assures both temporal and eternal truth. Were it not so we would live in a world without knowledge or standards of any sort.

Truth 7

As there is only one Atonement and one Savior, there can only be one true Church.

8

Who can speak for God?

The historical Christian world knows nothing of priesthood and its operations in the salvation of man. The Bible, as we now have it, neither defines nor explains priesthood. True it is that there are biblical passages that evidence the priesthood but they can only be seen and understood by those who already know and understand the functioning of the priesthood. Without the light of the Restoration we would not see them.

When Martin Luther broke with the Roman Church, those he criticized revoked the authority by which he acted and claimed him to be without priesthood authority. His response was not a claim to such authority but rather that no such authority was needed. All, he argued, have within themselves the authority to do whatever is required of God. Such authority rested within the individual, not an organization. This is known as the priesthood of all believers and has become a fundamental doctrine of the Protestant faith.

While the Catholic faith professes a succession of the keys promised by Christ to Peter, no such conferral of keys takes place in practice. When the College of Cardinals meets to choose a new pope he is chosen from among their number. The man he succeeds made no personal conveyance of keys to him. His authority comes from the vote of his fellow cardinals, none of whom have any claim that such keys were ever given to them. Thus they are called on to give what they do not have.

Theological dictionaries and encyclopedias can be searched in vain for a Catholic definition of priesthood.

It is popular sport in the Evangelic world to point an accusing finger at Mormonism and make a great flap and fuss over the fact that we as Latter-day Saints did not give the priesthood to black members until 1978. What has not been asked is when they gave the priesthood to black individuals. The answer is that they have not. They, like Luther, eschew the necessity of authority and deny the need for any rites or ordinances. This is hypocrisy at its best. Surely it evidences no concern for black Church members to argue that we have discriminated against them by not giving to them what those with pointed fingers eschew themselves. Do you show interest in a friend by arguing that someone give them something you believe to be evil and that will only lead to their destruction?

What then do we understand the priesthood to be? It is the power and authority by which all the blessings of the Atonement are administered. Our revelation declares the high and holy priesthood to be the authority to administer the gospel (Doctrine and Covenants 84:19). "[It] is," said Joseph Smith, "the channel through which all knowledge, doctrine, the plan of salvation, and every important matter is revealed from heaven" (Teachings of the Prophet Joseph Smith, 167).

If God's house is a house of order it cannot be governed by laws of someone else's making; it will not honor offerings made to other gods, nor will ordinances performed without its permission or authority be accepted. Laws evidence the existence of God. The first command in the creation was, "Let there be light" (Genesis 1:3). That light is the gospel, which is administered by the priesthood.

Truth 8

Only those who possess the priesthood have the right to speak for God.

9

How does the keeping of records evidence that the Church is true?

During the meeting at which the Church was organized Joseph Smith received and dictated a revelation commanding that "there should be a record kept" containing the history of the Church (Doctrine and Covenants 21:1).

The Church of Jesus Christ of Latter-day Saints has a more complete and perfect history than any other organization of comparable size upon the face of the earth. Virtually without exception those events for which adequate records do not exist are the result of the persecution of the Saints, not their lack of discipline or obedience in keeping this commandment.

This is not the course a scoundrel takes. If Joseph Smith had in mind some self-aggrandizing scheme, as his critics are so wont to tell us, a record of his doings is the last thing in the world he would want.

Similarly, we would hardly expect him to warn against priestcrafts in the Book of Mormon. "For, behold, priestcrafts are that men preach and set themselves up for a light unto the world, that they may get gain and praise of the world; but they seek not the welfare of Zion" (2 Nephi 26:29).

Given that this newly formed church found it necessary to flee New York to Ohio, from Ohio to Missouri, from Missouri to Illinois and from Illinois to a desert wilderness well beyond the boundaries of the United States wanted by no one else, it would be hard to argue that we have ever done anything that pleases the world.

As to our history, it is there for all to see. We would that every honest soul read it. We but ask the privilege be extended to us to tell our own story and declare our own doctrines. It is only falsehood that seeks to deny another their day in court. What spirit would seek to silence the voice of an angel, the words of prophets, or the testimony of righteous men? What is there in the story of a fourteen-year-old boy that threatens the whole Christian world?

In the telling of his own story, Joseph Smith writes, "Owing to the many reports which have been put in circulation by evil-disposed and designing persons, in relation to the rise and progress of the Church of Jesus Christ of Latter-day Saints, all of which have been designed by the authors thereof to militate against its character as a Church and its progress in the world—I have been induced to write this history, to disabuse the public mind, and put all inquirers after truth in possession of the facts, as they have transpired, in relation both to myself and the Church, so far as I have such facts in my possession" (Joseph Smith—History 1:1).

Who among professing Christians would believe in Christ had their reading been restricted to the Gospels of Pilot, Herod, Judas, and Caiaphas? Yet, such is the standard by which Mormonism is judged.

Truth 9

One cannot understand the doctrines of the Restoration without first understanding the history that brought them forth. By divine command, from the day the Church was organized, a record has been kept and is available to all.

10
Does God have favorites?

Within the ordinances of salvation we find the perfect illustration of spiritual equality. The words of the baptismal prayer, the sacramental prayers, and all the ordinances of the temple, are to be rendered exactly as revealed. To none has God granted the right to add to or take from them. Thus the promises given to one are the promises given to all. From the greatest to the least, the rights of heavenly citizenship are the same.

The promise of the ordinances is the same in all gospel dispensations and among all peoples. The gospel requires no man to kneel to another; it recognizes no distinction as to gender or race. The hand of fellowship is extended to all alike, as is emphasized repeatedly in scripture.

"We believe that through the Atonement of Christ, all mankind may be saved, by obedience to the laws and ordinances of the Gospel" (Articles of Faith 1:3).

"He inviteth them all to come unto him and partake of his goodness; and he denieth none that come unto him, black and white, bond and free, male and female; and he remembereth the heathen; and all are alike unto God, both Jew and Gentile" (2 Nephi 26:33).

If we all have made the same covenants and are rightful heirs of the same promises, then we all have the same responsibility to keep the commandments. We have no right to expect our leaders to live a higher standard than we do. Salvation grows out of covenants not offices.

To the extent that any member of the Church has failed to keep the commandments, to that extent they have constrained the Spirit and the flow of heaven's blessings on the body of the Church. It was the city of Enoch, meaning its people, that were taken to heaven, not just its bishops and its stake presidents.

Truth 10

Beginning with Adam, all members of the Church stand on equal ground. All have made the same covenants and all receive the same promises. Agency assures everyone the right to accept or reject these blessings.

What's wrong with Bible religion?

All true religion is revealed religion. God stands revealed or remains forever unknown. Every doctrine we espouse must bear the label of revelation. Our testimony to all nations is that Joseph Smith instituted a new and final dispensation of the gospel. A dispensation is a period in which the doctrines of salvation are dispensed anew from the heavens. This means we feast upon the fruits of our own garden, not the record of what others ate. It means that when we go to General Conference we raise our right hand to the square to sustain living prophets, seers, and revelators, not Peter, James, and John. The Church does not rest upon a record of what the Lord said to others but rather on what he is saying to us. As the Lord gave keys to the ancients, all who held keys or authority necessary to our dispensation conferred their presidency upon us.

If every Bible on the face of the earth and all the knowledge contained therein were to disappear tomorrow, The Church of Jesus

Christ of Latter-day Saints would not skip a heartbeat. Every doctrine, ordinance, and authority necessary for the salvation of men has been restored to us anew in this the dispensation of the fullness of times.

All revelation must be immediate and personal. No man can be saved by another man's revelation. To argue that you can be saved by a revelation given to someone else is to argue that your sins are remitted by their baptism and that you will be crowned with glory because of what they did. You might as well argue that their spouse is your spouse and their children your children.

Joseph Smith is the pattern we are to follow in learning the gospel. We are to learn as he learned, and that was by the Spirit of Revelation. "The best way to obtain truth and wisdom is not to ask it from books, but to go to God in prayer, and obtain divine teaching" (*Teachings of the Prophet Joseph Smith*, 191).

The Bible when read without the Spirit of Revelation is nothing more than religious history. It is the power of the Holy Ghost as found in the reader that transforms it into scripture. As to those who are so quick to point out to us that their religion is Bible religion, we would note that Bible religion is unbiblical. No one who lived within the covers of the Bible had a Bible. What they had was living prophets and the Spirit of Revelation. All anti-Mormon arguments reduce themselves to the same thing: the critics' refusal to accept the principle of revelation.

Scripture, which is the mind and will of God, cannot be scripture in the hands of an evil spirit. The Spirit must always light the torch of truth before it can give light. The word of God, which is light and truth, is a living thing. It cannot cease to be true and it cannot cease to give off light. All revelation by its very nature begets more revelation. Everything that lives produces in its own image and likeness. This is the eternal order of things.

Truth 11

The Lord never had a people that he acknowledged as his own, to whom he would not speak, or to whom he would not give the Spirit of Revelation.

12
What happened to the 12 Apostles?

When Christ commenced his ministry in the Old World he created a quorum of twelve men called and ordained to be Apostles. The same pattern was followed in the New World when he appeared to the Nephites. He told them that he was going to visit the lost tribes of Israel, and we assume he followed the same pattern among them. Again, in our dispensation, as soon as the Church was large enough to bear it, a quorum of twelve Apostles was formed. The office and call of an Apostle is to be a "special [witness] of the name of Christ in all the world" (Doctrine and Covenants 107:23).

In each instance this quorum was twelve in number, and so we ask the question, "Why? Could they not have been a quorum of ten, seven or some other number?" The answer is an unequivocal no. The twelve Apostles represented the twelve princes of the tribes of Israel and thus stood as living witness that the Lord had not forgotten the promises he made anciently to gather their tribes and return them to the power and majesty of the covenant made with their fathers.

It is the Book of Mormon that unlocks the full meaning of what is involved here. On the title page Moroni announces that the purpose of the book is "to show unto the remnant of the House of Israel what great things the Lord hath done for their fathers; and that they may know the covenants of the Lord." Then comes the promise that Jew and Gentile might know that Jesus is the Christ. Many have not recognized that the sequence of events as given here by Moroni is absolutely necessary to properly understanding them.

Moroni said the scattered remnants of Israel must first come to the knowledge of the covenants the Lord made with their fathers and then they will be graced with the knowledge that Jesus is the Christ. The principle here involved is that covenants precede knowledge. For instance, baptism precedes receiving the gift of the Holy Ghost. The Holy Ghost is a revelator. The sure revelation that Jesus is the Christ is only granted to those who enjoy this gift.

Nephi taught this principle to his brothers in this language: "And at that day shall the remnant of our seed know that they are of the house of Israel, and that they are the covenant people of the Lord; and then shall they know and come to the knowledge of their forefathers, and also to the knowledge of the gospel of their Redeemer, which was ministered unto their fathers by him; wherefore, they shall come to the knowledge of their Redeemer and the very points of his doctrine, that they may know how to come unto him and be saved" (1 Nephi 15:14).

Nephi's reasoning is the same as Moroni's. You must come to a knowledge of your fathers, and then you must come to the knowledge of the covenant God made with them. This is knowledge that can be had only by participating in the same covenants they did. The covenant in turn unlocks to you knowledge of the Redeemer and the "very points of his doctrine" that you might know how to be saved.

This means that the knowledge of salvation grows out of covenants and can be had in no other way. Teaching this same principle, Mormon said, "And as surely as the Lord liveth, will he gather in from the four quarters of the earth all the remnant of the seed of Jacob, who are scattered abroad upon all the face of the earth.

"And as he hath covenanted with all the house of Jacob, even so shall the covenant wherewith he hath covenanted with the house of Jacob be fulfilled in his own due time, unto the restoring all the house of Jacob unto the knowledge of the covenant that he covenanted with them.

"And then shall they know their Redeemer, who is Jesus Christ, the Son of God; and then shall they be gathered in from the four quarters of the earth unto their own lands, from whence they have been dispersed; yea, as the Lord liveth so shall it be. Amen" (3 Nephi 5:24–26).

The Book of Mormon prophets clearly taught that Christ could be known only through covenants. Thus the Lord calls the Book of Mormon the "new covenant" (Doctrine and Covenants 84:57). The final commission given by Christ to the meridian Twelve was to go into all the world teaching and "baptizing them in the name of the Father, and of the Son, and of the Holy Ghost" (Matthew 28:19). The gathering of Israel consists of the baptizing of Israel. Lehi's son Jacob stated the matter thus: "And now, my beloved brethren, I have read these things that ye might know concerning the covenants of the Lord that he has covenanted with all the house of Israel—

"That he has spoken unto the Jews, by the mouth of his holy prophets, even from the beginning down, from generation to generation, until the time comes that they shall be restored to the true church and fold of God; when they shall be gathered home to the lands of their inheritance, and shall be established in all their lands of promise" (2 Nephi 9:1–2).

This is the commission given to the Twelve of our day (Doctrine and Covenants 18:27–28). They are to declare the new and everlasting covenant, meaning baptism and all ordinances that follow, among all nations and peoples, for the keys of these ordinances rest with them. Without them there can be no true and living Church, nor can the saving knowledge of Christ exist.

Truth 12

Distinctive to The Church of Jesus Christ of Latter-day Saints is the Quorum of Twelve Apostles. They alone, have the same commission as their ancient counterparts to declare the name of Christ among all nations and to exercise the same gifts and powers.

13

What is the promise of the Word of Wisdom?

The revelation known to Latter-day Saints as the Word of Wisdom is frequently cited as an evidence that Joseph Smith is a prophet. Indeed, it evidences the point but for a much better reason than is generally supposed. There is much more taking place in this revelation than God manifesting his concern that we care properly for our bodies. As Latter-day Saints we are alone in worshiping a God who has such concerns (Doctrine and Covenants 89).

To understand the revelation let us thoughtfully consider the following:

Question: To whom is the revelation given?

Answer: The revelation is addressed to the council of high priests assembled in Kirtland and to others throughout the Church. Among this group was what we know as the School of the Prophets. It would appear that there is a relationship between obtaining knowledge of the things of the kingdom and the manner in which we care for the physical tabernacle that houses our spirit.

The language of the revelation then extends itself to "all saints in the last days" and states that it is "adapted to the capacity of the weak, and the weakest of saints, who are or can be called saints" (Doctrine and Covenants 89:2–3).

Question: If those not of our faith live the principles announced in the Word of Wisdom will they receive the same blessings?

Answer: No. This will become increasingly clear as the revelation continues, but to suppose that blessings promised to those who have faith in God can be enjoyed by the faithless negates the need for both faith and God.

The revelation then continues to state the taboos, or restrictions, on the Saints. We are not to use wine or "strong drink," which is biblical language for alcoholic beverages, and we are not to use tobacco or hot drinks. Hot drinks were understood in that day to mean tea and coffee. The issue was not the temperature at which they were taken but the addictive drugs they contained. Some have used this as an excuse to drink Cola drinks that do not have caffeine in them. To do so rather misses the spirit of the law. No grandfather wants to have his grandchildren catch him drinking decaffeinated coffee. As we shall see the letter of the law is very closely associated with the spirit of the law.

The taboos are followed by an announcement of the things God created for the use of man, which include "all grains," "fruit of the vine," "the fowls of heaven," and "wild animals," which we are told are particularly for times of "famine" or "excess of hunger" (Doctrine and Covenants 89:14–16).

Following this comes the promise—that "all saints" who live this temporal law while walking in obedience to the fullness of the gospel law shall receive "health in their navel and marrow to their bones" and shall find "wisdom and great treasures of knowledge, even hidden treasures" (Doctrine and Covenants 89:18–19). It is obedience to the temporal law that unlocks the blessings of the spiritual law.

The matter of great import here is not that Latter-day Saints live longer than non-Latter-day Saints. It is not that fewer of them will get cancer than their Gentile neighbors. It is found in the purpose for which they live. This revelation—lived in concert with all gospel principles—gives the Saints the power to unlock the heavens and know what the Lord would have them do and be. The revelation states that they "shall find wisdom and great treasures of knowledge, even hidden treasures; and shall run and not be weary, and shall walk and not faint" (Doctrine and Covenants 89:19–20).

Those so blessed are "sanctified by the Spirit unto the renewing of their bodies" (Doctrine and Covenants 84:33). We have a wonderful text in Isaiah that helps us understand what is involved here:

"Hast thou not known? Hast thou not heard, that the everlasting God, the LORD, the Creator of the ends of the earth, fainteth not, neither is weary? There is no searching of his understanding.

"He giveth power to the faint; and to them that have no might he increaseth strength.

"Even the youths shall faint and be weary, and the young men shall utterly fall:

"But they that wait upon the LORD shall renew their strength; they shall mount up with wings as eagles; they shall run, and not be weary; and they shall walk, and not faint" (Isaiah 40:28–31).

The Word of Wisdom concludes with the promise that as the destroying angel passed over the children of Israel who had marked the inlets of their doors with the blood of the Lamb, so the Saints would be spared destruction in the last days. The revelation represents a sacred covenant with Christ (Exodus 12).

As the covenant spokesman for our day, Joseph Smith, in this revelation, shows us how to obtain the keys of knowledge and the plan of salvation in a manner that cannot otherwise be had or experienced. Indeed, it is our invitation to join the School of the Prophets and have the heavens opened to us as they were to the ancients. The plan of salvation was not created for a select few. If the promise of scripture was intended for one person alone we would need only one copy of the Bible.

Truth 13

Joseph Smith is the only prophet in earth's history to record a revelation that is both a health law and a promise to the Saints that the mysteries of the kingdom will be revealed to them. Such promises are not espoused in any other church.

14
Does grace need works?

When I served as a chaplain in Vietnam, the Reverend Billy Graham made a visit to bring salvation to the soldiers in that war-torn country. My responsibility as a Chaplain was to see that every man in the unit to which I was assigned who wanted to attend his revival had the opportunity to do so. A place was chosen for the revival and the soldiers gathered. They came in large convoys from many units in open trucks and on armored personnel carriers. They wore full battle dress. Helicopters made regular passes along our convoy lines and perimeter guards were quickly stationed. Everything was done that could be done to ensure the safety of our soldiers. Reverend Graham granted a special dispensation that day, given our battle front position. Those who chose to be saved needed only bow their heads and raise their arms at the appointed moment. Whether I chose to do so or not I leave to the discretion of the reader, but it was all that was required that day to obtain a sure place in kingdom of God.

Some years later when I served in Scotland as a mission president, I was accosted one morning upon arriving at the chapel at which we were holding a zone conference by a car full of loud and mean-spirited young men who had come to welcome me with the news that I, and all who believed as I did, were to be damned to the lowest possible depths of hell. The reason for our unconditional ban from heavenly realms was that we were attempting to emulate the life of Christ and do good works.

It seemed a strange distinction to me. I had been offered salvation through the profession of faith and the outward act of raising my arm. Now I had been damned for conscious efforts to live a Christlike life and for my efforts to keep his commandments.

Why, I was left to wonder, did Christ devote himself to the love and service of others if it is so offensive to the spirit of the heaven he has created for us?

What, then, is the doctrine of grace and its relationship to works as it has been revealed to us? Let us take the act of childbirth as an illustration of the principle herein involved.

The conception of a child requires both a father and a mother. Even the most sincere effort on the part of a man or woman to sire a child without the aid of a companion of the opposite sex will fail. So it is with all gospel principles: there is none of their number that has the power to give life acting separately and singly. Any gospel principle placed in isolation from its companion principles becomes corrupted and distorted in its isolation. It ceases to be a correct principle.

It is for this reason that there is no divine grace without works, nor can there be acceptable works that are independent of the principle of grace. Scripture provides no more perfect illustration than Nephi's dream wherein he had the true meaning of the tree of life unfolded to him. Invited to the high mountain that he might hear and see and ask what it was he desired to know, he said it would be to understand the meaning of the tree which his father had been shown. His request evoked a question from the angel who acted as his guide. The angel asked Nephi if he knew the meaning of the tree. Nephi was then shown a vision of a most beautiful virgin who brought forth a son, and the angel asked, "Knowest thou the condescension of God?" Not being fully sure of himself, the youthful Nephi responded, "I know that he loveth his children: nevertheless, I do not know the meaning of all things" (1 Nephi 11:1–7).

How would you or I have responded to the same question? To condescend is to voluntarily lower one's self to a station beneath that normally expected. Were a God to condescend he would do something gods just normally do not do. There is no condescension in God loving his child as Nephi suggests. All parents love their children. The answer is found in his siring a child in the flesh, the fathering of a child with a mortal mother, a child thus unlike all the other children of the divine Father, one who would be subject to death, having a mortal mother. Thus we speak of God's condescension and of a plan of salvation that requires a son of God to be born with both the power to lay down his life and to take it up again in a resurrected and immortal state. Thus our text reads: "And he said unto me: Behold, the virgin whom thou seest is the mother of the Son of God, after the manner of the flesh.

"And it came to pass that I beheld that she was carried away in the Spirit; and after she had been carried away in the Spirit for the space of a time the angel spake unto me, saying: Look!

"And I looked and beheld the virgin again, bearing a child in her arms.

"And the angel said unto me: Behold the Lamb of God, yea even the Son of the Eternal Father! Knowest thou the meaning of the tree which thy father saw?

"And I answered him, saying: Yea, it is the love of God, which sheddeth itself abroad in the hearts of the children of men; wherefore, it is the most desirable above all things" (1 Nephi 11:18–22).

Then Nephi's angelic guide asked again if he understood the condescension of God, referring this time to the events of Christ's mortal ministry and how he would be lifted up on a cross and slain for the sins of the world (1 Nephi 11:26–33). So we have a second great act of condescension or grace taking place and we recognize that they cannot be divided from each other but require the labor of two Gods, the Father and the Son.

The grace of the Father and the Son consisted in their condescending to do for us what we could not do for ourselves. No one can give birth to themselves. Further, we are without the power to raise ourselves from the dead or to create our own celestial kingdom. Any who possess such powers are without the need of divine help; they have no need for God, for Christ, for the Atonement, or for any of the principles constituting the plan of salvation, for they have nothing to be saved from.

It would be equally true that if our good works could save us that salvation would be of our own making. Obedience to laws of some unknown making would confer upon them the blessings of salvation and again we would find ourselves in the position of needing no help save the laws we had ordained for that purpose.

But what then is the need and place for works? In a marvelous revelation given to the Prophet Joseph Smith, John the Baptist explains how it was that Christ advanced from grace to grace (Doctrine and Covenants 93:11–13). It was required of him that he constantly improve, that he do as prophets have commanded us to do—and that is to add to his virtue knowledge, and to his knowledge temperance, and to his temperance patience, and to his patience brotherly kindness, and to his brotherly kindness godliness, and to his godliness charity, and to his charity humility, and to his humility diligence (Doctrine and Covenants 4:6).

Truth 14

The revelations of the Restoration teach of an inseparable relationship between the grace of God—that which we cannot do for ourselves—and our laboring to advance from grace to grace through godly works, thus taking two doctrines the world has placed at odds and making them one.

15
Why the law of witnesses?

As part of the restoration of all things Joseph Smith restored the ancient law of witnesses. This law holds that "In the mouth of two or three witnesses shall every word be established" (2 Corinthians 13:1). This is not a principle you institute if you have reason to hide anything.

In harmony with this law, Joseph Smith was never alone when either priesthood or its keys were restored. When John the Baptist came to restore the Aaronic Priesthood and its keys Joseph Smith and Oliver Cowdery were together. The same pattern was followed in the restoration of the Melchizedek Priesthood (Joseph Smith—History 1:68–72). Still again, when Moses restored the keys of the gathering of Israel, Elias "the dispensation of the gospel of Abraham," and Elijah the keys of the sealing power, Joseph and Oliver were together (Doctrine and Covenants 110:11–16).

It was this law that required both Joseph Smith and his brother Hyrum to seal their testimony with their blood in Carthage Jail. When they were killed two other Apostles were with them, John Taylor and Willard Richards. In the providence of God their lives were spared that there might be two apostolic witnesses to tell the story.

The Book of Mormon stands as a second witness to the Bible. Speaking to those who declare the Bible to be sufficient the Lord said: "Wherefore murmur ye, because that ye shall receive more of my word? Know ye not that the testimony of two nations is a witness unto you that I am God, that I remember one nation like unto another? And when the two nations shall run together the testimony of the two nations shall run together also" (2 Nephi 29:8).

In Second Nephi we also read this prophecy: "Wherefore, at that day when the book shall be delivered unto the man of whom I have spoken, the book [meaning the plates] shall be hid from the eyes of the world, that the eyes of none shall behold it save it be that three witnesses shall behold it, by the power of God, besides him to whom the book shall be delivered; and they shall testify to the truth of the book and the things therein.

"And there is none other which shall view it, save it be a few according to the will of God, to bear testimony of his word unto the children of men; for the Lord God hath said that the words of the faithful should speak as if it were from the dead" (2 Nephi 27:12–13).

As Moroni concludes that which was written on the plates he returned to this promise, saying: "And unto three shall they be shown by the power of God; wherefore they shall know of a surety that these things are true.

"And in the mouth of three witnesses shall these things be established; and the testimony of three, and this work, in the which shall be shown forth the power of God and also the word, of which the Father, and the Son, and the Holy Ghost bear record—and all this shall stand as a testimony against the world at the last day" (Ether 5:3–4).

In June of 1829, a detailed revelation was given relative to what the three witnesses would be shown. "And it is by your faith that you shall obtain a view of them, even by that faith which was had by the prophets of old" (Doctrine and Covenants 17:2).

The reader is reminded that every copy of the Book of Mormon contains the testimony of the three witnesses, in which the witnesses state that they were shown the plates from which the Book of Mormon was translated by "an angel of God." Each copy of the Book of Mormon also contains the testimony of eight witnesses stating that they too, had seen the plates.

Thus we have the testimony of twelve men: Joseph Smith, the three witnesses, and the eight other witnesses all testified that they had seen the plates. The number twelve is the perfect expression of the law of witnesses.

The Godhead, which consists of three separate and distinct persons, also provides a perfect illustration of the law of witnesses. Teaching this Christ stated:

"And this is my doctrine, and it is the doctrine which the Father hath given unto me; and I bear record of the Father, and the Father beareth record of me, and the Holy Ghost beareth record of the Father and me; and I bear record that the Father commandeth all men, everywhere, to repent and believe in me. . . .

"Verily, verily, I say unto you, that this is my doctrine, and I bear record of it from the Father; and whoso believeth in me believeth in the Father also; and unto him will the Father bear record of me, for he will visit him with fire and with the Holy Ghost.

"And thus will the Father bear record of me, and the Holy Ghost will bear record unto him of the Father and me; for the Father, and I, and the Holy Ghost are one" (3 Nephi 11:32, 35–36).

This heavenly presidency of three establishes the pattern for all that happens in the Church. It is presided over by a presidency of three, as is every stake and ward auxiliary. No one is ever invited to act in truth alone. A church that has a man or woman standing at its head, acting alone, cannot be the Lord's.

Truth 15

The restoration of the law of witnesses, long lost to the historical Christian world, is an eloquent testimony that Joseph Smith was a prophet.

16
Whose Church is it?

How could one suppose that they were a member of the Church founded by Christ if their church did not bear his name? If a church bears the name of a country, like the Church of England, for instance, then it is the church of that country and belongs to that country's monarch, who will call its leaders and determine its doctrines and its ordinances.

I will use the ordinance of marriage to illustrate the point. As a chaplain in the Army of the United States I performed marriages by the authority of that office. The greatest army in the world had commissioned me to act as its agent in the performance of this ordinance. As a Latter-day Saint bishop I performed marriages by the authority of the state of Utah and as a mission president in Scotland I performed a marriage by the authority of the Queen of England. However, as a temple sealer I have performed marriages by the authority of the sealing power held by the prophet and seer of the Lord which was conferred upon me under the hands of a member of the Quorum of the Twelve Apostles which he did under the direction of the President of the Church. In the first three instances I acted to the extent of the authority I had been given and pronounced the couple married "until death did them part." Only as a temple sealer could I use the words "for time and for all eternity."

The doctrine here involved is revealed to us in a beautiful story found in the ministry of Christ to his newly called disciples in the New World. After his visit among them they commenced to travel throughout the land teaching and baptizing. As they did so they found that there was contention among the members of the Church over the matter of what its name should be. This may have resulted from the ending of the dispensation of Moses and the beginning of the new dispensation under the hands of Christ himself. To answer the question the Twelve Apostles, for so Moroni called them, united together in fasting and prayer. As they prayed Christ appeared in the midst of them and inquired as to what they desired that he give them. They rehearsed the question asked in their prayer to which Christ responded with two rhetorical questions:

"Have they not read the scriptures, which say ye must take upon you the name of Christ, which is my name? For by this name shall ye be called at the last day;

"And whoso taketh upon him my name, and endureth to the end, the same shall be saved at the last day.

"Therefore, whatsoever ye shall do, ye shall do it in my name; therefore ye shall call the church in my name; and ye shall call upon the Father in my name that he will bless the church for my sake.

"And how be it my church save it be called in my name? For if a church be called in Moses' name then it be Moses' church; or if it be called in the name of a man then it be the church of a man; but if it be called in my name then it is my church, if it so be that they are built upon my gospel" (3 Nephi 27:5–8).

If a church be called in the name of Luther then it is Luther's church, this is but part of the story. There are parts of our own country that are dotted with churches both large and small. Out in front of each of them is a billboard of one sort or another announcing the name of person or community whose church it is. When one passes a meetinghouse of The Church of Jesus Christ of Latter-day Saints, the cornerstone of the building will announce its name. The name of the bishop never appears, for it is not his church, nor will one ever see a clever one-liner about the sermon that will be preached, for we do not set one bishop against another to compete for membership and tithing dollars.

The principle here stated is the same in community churches. The minister serves at their bidding. It is the same in national churches and all churches of men. The churches of men belong to men and are governed by rules and practices of their own making.

It is the common practice in countries where church and state have joined hands to ban the teaching of the Restored gospel. If you do not accept their creeds you cannot teach in their nation. We cannot send missionaries to many nations of the earth for this reason. The Church of Jesus Christ of Latter-day Saints is the Lord's church. He runs it, he reveals its doctrines, he calls its officers, and he directs the course they take in his name.

Truth 16
The Lord's Church must bear his name and all that is done within or by the Church must bear his name.

Was this work "done in a corner"?

The phrase I have chosen for the title of this chapter comes from Paul in his defense of the gospel before King Agrippa. The point Paul was making was that the prophecy and events that surrounded the restoration of the gospel in that day were known to many, they did not take place in hidden meetings or behind closed doors. As it was with the restoration of Christianity in that day so it was in our day. No prophet has ever been as open to the view of others as Joseph Smith.

Parley P. Pratt, who was present when several revelations were received, described the process thus: "Each sentence was uttered slowly and very distinctly, and with a pause between each, sufficiently long for it to be recorded by an ordinary writer, in long hand. This was the manner in which all his written revelations were dictated and written. There was never any hesitation, reviewing or reading back, in order to keep the run of the subject" (*Autobiography of Parley P. Pratt*, 48).

William E. McClellin, in like manner, said, "I, as scribe, have written revelations from the mouth of [the Prophet]. And I have been present many times when others wrote for Joseph; therefore I speak as one having experience. The scribe seats himself at a desk or table, with pen, ink, and paper. The subject of enquiry being understood, the Prophet and Revelator enquires of God. He spiritually sees, hears, and feels, and then speaks as he is moved upon by the Holy Ghost, the 'thus saith the Lord,' sentence after sentence, and waits for his amanuenses to write and then read aloud each sentence. Thus they proceed until the revelator says Amen, at the close of what is then communicated. I have known [Joseph], without premeditation, to thus deliver off in broken sentences, some of the most sublime pieces of composition which I ever perused in any book" (Backman, Milton V., and Richard O. Cowan, *Joseph Smith and the Doctrine and Covenants*, 1–2).

Of Joseph Smith, Elder Bruce R. McConkie said, "Here is a man who has given to our present world more holy scripture than any single prophet who ever lived; indeed, he has preserved for us more of the mind and will and voice of the Lord than the total of the dozen most prolific prophetic phenomenon of the past" (Conference Report, April 1976).

Virtually every revelation recorded in the Doctrine and Covenants was received and recorded in the presence of others. Philo Dibble illustrates the matter with this interesting account of the manner Joseph Smith and Sidney received the great revelation on the degrees of glory. He writes as follows: "Joseph would, at intervals, say: 'What do I see?' Then he would relate what he had seen or what he was looking at. Then Sidney replied, 'I see the same.' Presently Sidney would say, 'What do I see?' . . . and would repeat what he had seen or was seeing, and Joseph would reply, 'I see the same.' This manner of conversation was repeated at short intervals to the end of the vision, and during the whole time not a word was spoken by any other person. Not a sound nor motion made by anyone but Joseph and Sidney, and it seemed to me that they never moved a joint or limb during the time I was there, which I think was over an hour, and to the end of the vision."

"Joseph sat firmly and calmly all the time in the midst of a magnificent glory, but Sidney sat limp and pale, apparently as limber as a rag, observing which, Joseph remarked, smilingly, 'Sidney is not used to it as I am'" (Dibble, Philo, "Recollections of the Prophet Joseph Smith," 304).

Introducing the compilation of revelations contained in the Doctrine and Covenants, the Lord invited all to taste of their goodness.

"Search these commandments, for they are true and faithful, and the prophecies and promises which are in them shall all be fulfilled.

"What I the Lord have spoken, I have spoken, and I excuse not myself; and though the heavens and the earth pass away, my word shall not pass away, but shall all be fulfilled, whether by mine own voice or by the voice of my servants, it is the same" (Doctrine and Covenants 1:37–38).

Truth 17

When the Lord raises up a prophet he also raises up those who will stand at his side and echo the truthfulness of what he taught. The Lord's work is never "done in a corner"—the Prophet Joseph did not stand alone.

18
How do we define resurrection?

The perfect evidence that salvation rests in Jesus Christ is found in his resurrection. Critics explain away his teachings and his miracles, but if in fact he broke the bands of death and thereby made immortality and eternal life possible, all efforts to deny him fail and he is indeed the Son of God and the Savior of all humankind.

The Christian world, while divided on a great host of issues, all of one accord unite to proclaim the resurrection of Christ. What is singularly significant is that none of its churches or denominations can tell us what the resurrection is. Is it not the obligation of the true Church to correctly define and teach what the resurrection is? If there is uncertainty on this doctrine of what can we be certain?

Dictionaries uniformly define the resurrection as the calling one forth from death to life. If this is what resurrection is then Lazarus should have lived forever and Christ was not the first fruits of the resurrection as scripture proclaims.

I have heard a rabbi define resurrection as the memory of us that our family and friends will carry in their minds. As the reader will note there is no need of Christ in such a definition.

In discussing the resurrection, most religious leaders cite the words of Paul wherein he said that in the resurrection we will have "a spiritual body" (1 Corinthians 15:44). Some interpret this to mean that we will return to the spirit essence from which we were made and become a drop of essence in the great ocean of essences. All seem united in the belief that gender will no longer exist and that marriage and family serve no purpose and will therefore not exist either. If we can trust the expressions common to obituaries, their doctrinal expressions fall on deaf ears and people much prefer to rest their faith in the scripture of the heart, which suggests quite the opposite to them.

In fairness to the world of Bible believers, we as Latter-day Saints would have no more knowledge than they if not for that which was revealed through Joseph Smith. The word resurrection is not mentioned in the Old Testament and is not defined in the New Testament. For a perfect definition we turn to the words of Alma:

"Now, behold, I have spoken unto you concerning the death of the mortal body, and also concerning the resurrection of the mortal body. I say unto you that this mortal body, is raised to an immortal body, that is from death unto life, that they can die no more; their spirits uniting with their bodies, never to be divided; thus the whole becoming spiritual and immortal, that they can no more see corruption" (Alma 11:45).

We know that death is the separation of the body and the spirit. We learn from Alma that in the resurrection they are united together "never to be divided." You cannot be resurrected and die again. We also learn that the phrase "spiritual body" as used by Paul means that the resurrected being can never again be subject to that which is temporal. This is the kind of body that Adam and Eve had before the Fall (Moses 3:7). Alma also tells us that the resurrected body can no more "see corruption," meaning that it cannot age or experience sickness of any kind.

In the vision of the redemption of the dead Joseph F. Smith describes that for which those assembled in the paradise of God waited:

"Their sleeping dust was to be restored unto its perfect frame, bone to his bone, and the sinews and the flesh upon them, the spirit and the body to be united never again to be divided, that they might receive a fulness of joy" (Doctrine and Covenants 138:17).

Not only does this passage affirm Alma's testimony that the union of body and spirit is such that it can "never again" be divided, but it also affirms that the phrase "sleeping dust" is not to be taken literally. Our spirits do not return to dust having no consciousness after death, as many as many so-called Bible believers have told us, but rather is a figurative phrase not meant to discount the manner in which life continues in the world of the spirits.

Two more texts can be cited to complete our definition of resurrection—one from old scripture and one from new. Alma also declared, "The soul shall be restored to the body, and the body to the soul; yea, and every limb and joint shall be restored to its body; yea, even a hair of the head shall not be lost; but all things shall be restored to their proper and perfect frame" (Alma 40:23).

The doctrine of resurrection as restored through the Prophet Joseph Smith holds that all things were given birth first as spirits and then granted physical tabernacles in the flesh, and that after their death they will be resurrected to inherit eternal glory.

When our revelation states that all things were created "spiritually, before they were naturally upon the face of the earth," it is referring to the fact that in their creation both as spirits and as physical beings they were not subject to death. It is the Fall that introduced death (Moses 3:5, 9).

This means that in the resurrection elephants will be elephants and bears will be bears, that eagles will be eagles and pigeons will be pigeons, that whales will be whales and salmon will be salmon, and that men will be men and women will be women, with the sanctified among them granted the power to give birth to those of their own species (Doctrine and Covenants 77:3). A church cannot be held to be true that cannot declare the doctrine of the resurrection. This doctrine plucked from the tree of paradise gives birth to a thousand other doctrines.

Truth 18

It is only in the revelations of the Restoration that we find a definition of the resurrection.

19

What is the seedbed of all saving truths?

It is not the practice of false prophets or the churches of the world to teach the doctrine of repentance. The doctrines that we most commonly hear are that we just shift the burden of our guilt to Christ, whose grace excuses all, or we make confession to a priest who forgives us and in some instances imposes upon us some duty or act of contrition to perform. In past centuries this often took place in the form of pilgrimages to holy sites or the taking up of the sword against the enemies of the faith.

In sharp contrast, Joseph Smith, speaking for the Lord, wrote as follows: "Therefore, I command you to repent—repent, lest I smite you by the rod of my mouth, and by my wrath, and by my anger, and your sufferings be sore—how sore you know not, how exquisite you know not, yea, how hard to bear you know not.

"For behold, I, God, have suffered these things for all, that they might not suffer if they would repent;

"But if they would not repent they must suffer even as I;

"Which suffering caused myself, even God, the greatest of all, to tremble because of pain, and to bleed at every pore, and to suffer both body and spirit—and would that I might not drink the bitter cup, and shrink" (Doctrine and Covenants 19:15–18).

The promise that the repentant soul would not be called upon to suffer as Christ had suffered was not intended to suggest that repentance would not then require any suffering on the part of those seeking its cleansing power. Alma made this clear, writing as follows: "Now, repentance could not come unto men except there were a punishment, which also was eternal as the life of the soul should be, affixed opposite to the plan of happiness, which was as eternal also as the life of the soul.

"Now, how could a man repent except he should sin? How could he sin if there was no law? How could there be a law save there was a punishment?

"Now there was a punishment affixed, and a just law given, which brought remorse of conscience unto man" (Alma 42:16–18).

So even though the repentant soul turns to Christ, the law of the gospel requires that they too must suffer. Elder Dallin Oaks used this illustration of this principle: "Why is it necessary for us to suffer on the way to repentance for serious transgressions? We often think of the results of repentance as simply cleansing us from sin. But that is an incomplete view of the matter. A person who sins is like a tree that bends easily in the wind. On a windy and rainy day the tree bends so deeply against the ground that the leaves become soiled with mud, like sin. If we only focus on cleaning the leaves, the weakness in the tree that allowed it to bend and soil its leaves may remain. Merely cleaning the leaves does not strengthen the tree. Similarly, a person who is merely sorry to be soiled by sin will sin again in the next high wind. The susceptibility to repetition continues until the tree has been strengthened.

"When a person has gone through the process that results in what the scriptures call a broken heart and a contrite spirit, that person is not only eligible to be cleansed from sin. He is also strengthened, and that strengthening is essential for us to realize the purpose of the cleansing, which is to return to our Heavenly Father. To be admitted to his presence we must be more than clean. We must also be changed from a weak person who once transgressed into a strong person with the spiritual stature that qualifies one to dwell in the presence of God. We must, as the scripture says, become 'a saint through the atonement of Christ the Lord' (Mosiah 3:19; also see Hafen, *The Broken Heart*, p. 149). This is what is meant by the scriptural explanation that a person who has repented of his sins will 'confess them and forsake them' (Doctrine and Covenants 58:43). Forsaking sins is more than resolving not to repeat them. It involves a fundamental change in the individual.

"King Benjamin and Alma both speak of 'a mighty change of heart.' King Benjamin's congregation described that mighty change by saying that they had "no more disposition to do evil, but to do good continually' (Mosiah 5:2). Alma illustrated that change of heart when he described a people who 'awoke unto God,' 'put their trust in' him, and were 'faithful until the end' (Alma 5:7, 13). He challenged others to 'look forward with an eye of faith' to the time when we will 'stand before God to be judged' according to our deeds. (Alma 5:15). Persons who have had that kind of change in their hearts have been cleansed from their sins and have attained the strength and stature to dwell with God. That is what we call being saved"(Dallin H. Oaks, "Sin and Suffering," BYU Devotional, 5 August 1990).

What then is the message we have been commissioned to take to all the earth? In a very real sense it is the doctrine of repentance. In revelations given to Joseph Smith and Oliver Cowdery the Lord repeatedly said to say "nothing but repentance" to those they taught (Doctrine and Covenants 6:9; 11:9; 18:13–15). Further defining what they were to teach the Lord said, "And of tenets thou shalt not talk, but thou shalt declare repentance and faith on the Savior, and remission of sins by baptism, and by fire, yea, even the Holy Ghost" (Doctrine and Covenants 19:31).

This is not to suggest that our message is confined to one subject and one subject alone, but rather we assert that no true principle can stand independent from the doctrine of repentance. Without repentance we cannot be baptized, without baptism we cannot receive the gift of the Holy Ghost, and without the gift of the Holy Ghost we cannot enjoy the Spirit of Revelation, which gives life and meaning to all gospel principles. It was clearly understood in ancient times that no unclean thing could enter into the presence of the Lord (Joseph Smith Translation, Exodus 33:20; Doctrine and Covenants 67:11–13).

There is no sin worth committing. True repentance embraces suffering. Repentance is a requisite part of all true religion. If a principle does not change behavior it is not of God.

Truth 19
All principles of the Restoration invite us to become more like God. As this is true of the doctrine of repentance it is equally true of all other gospel principles.

20

Can Christ's witnesses lack the Holy Ghost?

In sharing our message with others we do not argue and we do not seek to debate. Our commission is to teach and then testify that what we have taught is true. Our answers came from God and we invite all to check our source—let them ask of God as we have done and let them ponder the meaning of the revelations, as we have also done.

In his parting instruction to the Twelve in the Old World, Christ reviewed all that he had taught and showed them that he had fulfilled all that was required in the "law of Moses, and in the prophets, and in the psalms" concerning him. Thus he opened their minds that they "might understand the scriptures, and said unto them, Thus it is written, and thus it behoved Christ to suffer, and to rise from the dead the third day: And that repentance and remission of sins should be preached in his name among all nations, beginning in Jerusalem" (Luke 24:44–47).

Then came their apostolic charge, "Ye are witnesses of these things" (Luke 14:48). Two principles are involved here; they were to teach from the scriptures and show how Christ constituted their fulfillment, and then having so taught they were to seal their testimony with their personal witness. In effect they were to say, "These are the eyes with which I saw the resurrected Christ, and these are ears with which I heard him teach what I have taught, and these are the hands with which I felt the wounds in his side, and feet, and I testify that these things are true."

There is no room for argument here. The listener is free to accept or reject their testimony but they cannot argue with it.

Paul told us that no one can enjoy the companionship of the Holy Ghost and deny that Jesus is the Christ (Corinthians 12:3). In like manner, no one can deny that Joseph Smith is a prophet or that the revelations that came from him are not of God and have the Holy Ghost as their companion.

To those who sought to be witnesses of the revelations in the Doctrine and Covenants but wanted to quibble over some of the language in which the Prophet had clothed them, the Lord issued a challenge to write a better revelation. If they could not do it they were under obligation to testify that what was written was true (Doctrine and Covenants 67:3–7).

Who among the Prophet's critics has written a better book than the Book of Mormon? Who among their number has compiled a book that gives more light and knowledge on gospel principles than the Doctrine and Covenants? What does it say of them if their best criticism is to tell us that the heavens are sealed and that we cannot know what we know and cannot have what we have, for no better reason than they do not have it?

Truth 20

God gave us the Holy Ghost to teach and testify of truth. Evidence of that gift is found in all that we do in the restored Church.

21

Does God have a body?

We need look no further than the first chapter of Genesis to find one of the most sublime and beautiful passages of scripture ever penned. If it alone had survived the ravages of those who sought to take the plain and precious from the Holy Book it would have been worth the sacrifice of the countless martyrs who gave their lives that its sacred truths might be preserved. Yet the battle has not ended. While he failed to destroy the text, the prince of darkness has succeeded in veiling its meaning in a midst of darkness that keeps its readers from seeing and hearing what they are being told. For most the Bible remains a sealed book, for in its own words "they seeing see not, and hearing they hear not, neither do they understand" (Matthew 13:13).

In the creation story we read: "And God said, Let us make man in our image, after our likeness" (Genesis 1:26). The following verse affirms that this is what then took place. We read, "So God created man in his own image, in the image of God created he him; male and female created he them" (Genesis 1:27).

Two great questions demand answering. First, who is it that is called upon to aid God in the creative act, and second, what is to be understood by the expression "our own image and likeness"? Let us first consider the second of the two questions relative to "image and likeness," for it will aid us in understanding the answer to the first.

Clearly we are being told that God has both image and likeness as does his companion or companions in the act of creation. This is not some spirit essence of which we speak. The words do not permit the conclusion that the divine being of whom we read is a being without body or parts. Nor do they permit the conclusion that he cannot be seen. To have an image is to be seen, it is to be a person, and it is to have a body. All other scriptural texts that use this language support this conclusion. Thus we read, "This is the book of the generations of Adam. In the day that God created man, in the likeness of God made he him" (Genesis 5:1).

"In the image of his own body, male and female, created he them, and blessed them, and called their name Adam" (Moses 7:9).

"Behold, I am he who was prepared from the foundation of the world to redeem my people. Behold, I am Jesus Christ. I am the Father and the Son. In me shall all mankind have life, and that eternally, even they who shall believe on my name; and they shall become my sons and my daughters.

"And never have I showed myself unto man whom I have created, for never has man believed in me as thou hast. Seest thou that ye are created after mine own image? Yea, even all men were created in the beginning after mine own image" (Ether 3:14–15).

God, who cannot do that which is less than godly, did not create that which was inferior to himself. What glory could he take in such an act? What purpose would it serve? How would it advance the heavenly cause?

As God breathed life into the body of Adam so we breathed the light of heaven into the scriptural account by simply letting words mean what they say. To do so means that we read everything in the Bible by that light and we see the plan of salvation as the means whereby we progress to become as God is. This light is the key that unlocks our understanding to the three pillars of eternity: the Creation, the Fall, and the Atonement. To fail to do so is to rob these doctrines of their divine intent, making them prisoners of the creeds of men.

As Adam was created from the dust of the earth so was Eve, and so were you and so was I. Enoch, quoting from the writings of Adam, preserves this communication between Adam and God for us: "That by reason of transgression cometh the fall, which fall bringeth death, and inasmuch as ye [all mankind] were born into the world by water, and blood, and the spirit, which I have made, and *so become of dust a living soul,* even so ye must be born again into the kingdom of heaven, of water, and of the Spirit, and be cleansed by blood, even the blood of mine Only Begotten; that ye might be sanctified from all sin, and enjoy the words of eternal life in this world, and eternal life in the world to come, even immortal glory" (Moses 6:59, italics added).

The account of Eve's birth is most beautiful, particularly so in a day when there is so much confusion about the role of women. Symbolically, she was not taken from the bones of Adam's head or from the bones of his heel, for it not is the place of woman to be either above the man or beneath him. Her place is at his side, and so she is taken, in the figurative sense, from his rib—the bone that girds the side and rests closest to the heart. Thus we find Adam declaring: "This I know now is bone of my bones, and flesh of my flesh; she shall be called Woman, because she was taken out of man" (Moses 3:23). Eve, unlike the rest of God's creations, was of Adam's bone and of his flesh, meaning that she was equal to him in powers, faculties, and rights.

The official statement of the First Presidency on the Origin of Man, published in 1909, states: "It is held by some that Adam was not the first man upon the earth, and that the original human being was a development from lower orders of the animal creation. These, however, are the theories of men. The word of the Lord declares that Adam was the first man of all men (Moses 1:34), and we are, therefore, duty bound to regard him as the primal parent of our race. . . .

"The Church of Jesus Christ of Latter-day Saints, basing its belief on divine revelation, ancient and modern, proclaims man to be the direct and lineal offspring of Deity. . . . [God] formed every plant that grows, and every animal that breathes, each after its own kind spiritually and temporally—that which is spiritual being in the likeness of that which is temporal, and that which is temporal in the likeness of that which is spiritual. He made the tadpole and the ape, the lion and the elephant, but He did not make them in His own image, nor endow them with Godlike reason and intelligence. Nevertheless, the whole animal creation will be perfected and perpetuated in the Hereafter, each class in its 'distinct order or sphere,' and will enjoy 'eternal felicity.' That fact has been made plain in this dispensation."

Truth 21
It is only in the restored Church that we obtain an understanding of the importance of having received physical bodies from divine parents.

22

Who aided God in the creative act?

"So God created man in his own image, in the image of God created he him; male and female created he them" (Genesis 1:26–27). Of necessity we must answer, and answer well, the question as to whom God is speaking when he says, "Let *us* make man in our image, after our likeness." The generally accepted answer in the world of Jewish and Christian scholars is that God is conversing with lesser deities who constitute heaven's governing council. The answer accords harmoniously with Abraham's account of the creation where the text reads thus: "And the Gods took counsel among themselves and said: Let us go down and form man in our image, after our likeness; and we will give them dominion over the fish of the sea, and over the fowl of the air, and over the cattle, and over all the earth, and over every creeping thing that creepeth upon the earth.

"So the Gods went down to organize man in their own image, in the image of the Gods to form they him, male and female to form they them" (Abraham 4:26–27).

These Gods so spoken of do indeed form the heavenly council and are identified earlier in the text as the noble and great among the host of God's children who are yet to inhabit the earth (Abraham 3:21–22). They are referred to by President Joseph F. Smith in his vision of the redemption of the dead as "choice spirits" who even before they were born "received their first lessons in the world of spirits and were prepared to come forth in the due time of the Lord to labor in his vineyard for the salvation of the souls of men" (Doctrine and Covenants 138:53–56). According to this revelation they included "our glorious Mother Eve, with many of her faithful daughters" (Doctrine and Covenants 138:39). Thus the principle is set that all who live upon this earth lived before and are of the family of God. The Psalmist, describing this same scene, said, "God standeth in the congregation of the mighty; he judgeth among the gods." He concludes his thought with a reminder to us all, "Ye are gods; and all of you are children of the most High" (Psalm 82:1, 6).

As spirits we were fathered by the "most High" in heavenly realms long before we were born into this mortal sphere. "The Family: A Proclamation to the World" states the matter thus: "All human beings—male and female—are created in the image of God. Each is a beloved spirit son or daughter of heavenly parents, and, as such, each has a divine nature and destiny. Gender is an essential characteristic of individual premortal, mortal, and eternal identity and purpose."

Elder James E. Talmage described the matter thus: "We affirm as reasonable, scriptural, and true, the eternity of sex among the children of God. The distinction between male and female is no condition peculiar to the relatively brief period of mortal life. It was an essential characteristic of our pre-existent condition, even as it shall continue after death, in both disembodied and resurrected states. . . . [The] scriptures attest a state of existence preceding mortality, in which the spirit children of God lived, doubtless with distinguishing characteristics, including the distinction of sex, 'before they were [created] naturally upon the face of the earth'" ("The Eternity of Sex," *Millennial Star*, August 24, 1922, p. 530).

The man and the woman are part of each other. Neither of them stands complete separately and singly. It is evident from the very nature of their bodies that they were created to be together and that they were created to create, doing so after their own image and likeness.

We have also been taught, "Man in the fulness is a twofold organization—male and female. Either being incapable of filling the measure of their creation alone, it required the union of the two to complete man in the image of God, for in Genesis 1:27, it expressly says, that he was created male and female in the image of God. Therefore without the proper union of the sexes man would be less than what God created him to be" (Richards, Franklin D, and James A. Little, *A Compendium of the Doctrines of the Gospel*, 117).

It is fundamental to the truths of heaven to allow the word *father* to mean father, the word *son* to mean son, and the word *mother* to mean mother. We breathe the breath of life into the Bible by allowing words to mean what they say and say what they mean. It is the glory of God to bring to pass the immortality and eternal life of man (Moses 1:39).

Truth 22
The entire plan of salvation exists for the purpose of the perpetuation of the family unit. Salvation is a family affair, and it began with our divine parents.

23

How can we tell what is of God?

We cannot worship God in ignorance, falsehood, or error; there can be, as we have seen, only one true Church, and it must rest within the capacity of all who would worship the God of heaven to be able to discern between the truths of heaven and its countless counterfeits. In revelations unique to the Restored gospel we are told that all the sons and daughters of God born into this life are born with the Light of Christ, which light brings with it the power of discernment that none be confused or lost where eternal truths are concerned.

Moroni stated the principle in this manner: "For behold, the Spirit of Christ is given to every man, that he may know good from evil; wherefore, I show unto you the way to judge; for everything which inviteth to do good, and to persuade to believe in Christ, is sent forth by the power and gift of Christ; wherefore ye may know with a perfect knowledge it is of God" (Moroni 7:16).

It was not an uncommon experience as a mission president to have missionaries report spiritual experiences of one sort or another that their investigators claimed to be having. Some were of God and some were not. The missionaries question was always, "How do we discern them?" The answer is quite simple. They needed only to ask, "What was the purpose of this experience?" If it opened their heart to the message of salvation, if it encouraged them to exercise faith, to repent, and to be baptized, it was obviously of God. If, on the on the other hand it had as its purpose placing them above the law of the gospel and making them a law unto themselves whereby they were subject to no rules but those of their own making, the matter was quite simple.

Angels of the Lord do not come with a message from heaven that "all is well," that we need not do more, and that what we are doing is sufficient. Angels come because there is more to be done and they expect our help in getting it done. Indeed, the warning is that from those who say they have enough, or shall we add, say they are doing enough, from them "shall be taken away even that which they have" (2 Nephi 28:15–30).

The role of the Light of Christ is unfolded for us in Doctrine and Covenants 84:45-62. The pattern here established is that the Light of Christ teaches and leads to those things of a terrestrial order including great music, literature, art, science, and all that edifies and lifts the soul. This is but the precursor to receiving the fullness of the gospel message wherein our souls can be sanctified and we can receive those things that only come from the Holy Ghost and cannot be known to those who have not that gift.

When Moroni wrote the Book of Mormon's invitation to all who would read and ponder its pages, he promised, "And by the power of the Holy Ghost ye may know the truth of all things" (Moroni:10:5). He was not promising that we would in this mortal state be able to obtain all answers and thus have no need to walk by faith, but rather that we would be able know the truth when we heard it and discern it from error.

How singularly interesting it is that such promises are found only within the revelations of the Restoration and find no place in the theologies of men.

Truth 23

The greater the truth, the greater the heresy that will stand opposite it. All truth stands opposed. Satan never hollers about a doctrine he likes.

24

Does agency excuse or empower?

Joseph Smith consistently restored doctrines that deny a false prophet any place to hide. Chief among them is the doctrine of agency. No offering to God is acceptable save it be a free-will offering. There is simply no place in any gospel principle or ordinance for compulsion or force.

Agency reaches far beyond the right of choice; it is the power to act. Relatively few words have a single meaning. Like most other words, *agency* can be defined in a variety of ways for a variety of purposes. In the dictionary of Joseph Smith's day, which generally represents the meaning of words as they were used by the Prophet in the revelations of the Restoration, agency is defined as "exerting power" or the "state of being in action." An "agent" is defined as "one entrusted with the business of another," and an attorney or minister is used as an example. Current dictionaries preserve the same meaning.

Latter-day Saints generally think of agency as the right of choice.

Although agency includes the responsibility to make decisions, the focus of the word centers on the power of action and is thus broader in its application than simply making choices. The word *choice* is not used in dictionary definitions of agency.

The *Dictionary of Word Origins* tells us that a whole family of words has descended from the word *agent*, including such words as *act*, *action*, *active*, *actor*, and *actual*.

What addiction brings freedom to act? What commandments are we blessed for not keeping? No one has a God-given right to do what is wrong even if wrong has been done to them. Agency properly used always brings with it greater power and strength to do even greater good.

It is the purpose of the gospel to exalt humankind, not make robots out of them. The command is that we "serve [God] with all [our] heart, might, mind and strength" (Doctrine and Covenants 4:2). The might of both our heart and mind belong to God. To be created in his image and likeness is to have a mind capable of acting for itself.

"For behold, it is not meet that I should command in all things; for he that is compelled in all things, the same is a slothful and not a wise servant; wherefore he receiveth no reward.

"Verily I say, men should be anxiously engaged in a good cause, and do many things of their own free will, and bring to pass much righteousness;

"For the power is in them, wherein they are agents unto themselves. And inasmuch as men do good they shall in nowise lose their reward.

"But he that doeth not anything until he is commanded, and receiveth a commandment with doubtful heart, and keepeth it with slothfulness, the same is damned" (Doctrine and Covenants 58:26–29).

There is no requirement that we check our minds at the door of the chapel to be picked up again when the service ends. The proper use of the mind is a form of revelation.

It is the intent of God to reveal things to every baptized member of this Church and to reveal things through them. "I teach them correct principles," said the Prophet Joseph Smith, "and let them govern themselves." The Restoration is founded on the doctrine of agency, which is the right to do what is right and thus enhance every spiritual power within us.

> ## Truth 24
> Agency, a concept lost to the historical Christian world, assures the gospel will never embrace the doctrine of force. It will protect the mind and soul of man, particularly in our pursuit of righteousness.

25

Why is the knowledge of our premortal life important?

"I made the world," God told Moses, "and men before they were in the flesh" (Moses 6:51).

"And [I created] every plant of the field before it was in the earth, and every herb of the field before it grew. For I, the Lord God, created all things, of which I have spoken, spiritually, before they were naturally upon the face of the earth. . . . And I, the Lord God, had created all the children of men; and not yet a man to till the ground; for in heaven created I them; and there was not yet flesh upon the earth, neither in the water, neither in the air;

"But I, the Lord God, spake, and there went up a mist from the earth, and watered the whole face of the ground.

"And I, the Lord God, formed man from the dust of the ground, and breathed into his nostrils the breath of life; and man became a living soul, the first flesh upon the earth, the first man also; nevertheless, all things were before created; but spiritually were they created and made according to my word" (Moses 3:5–7).

In this text Adam is described in three distinct ways: as "a living soul," "the first flesh," and as "the first man." The phrases are not redundant. Each conveys an important truth about the nature of the man. Adam was the "firstborn." There were no pre-Adamites; among the entire pre-existent hosts he was the first to receive a physical body, the first to Fall, and thus the first to have blood course in his veins. It was the blood Fall that necessitated the blood Atonement. This made him the "first flesh," for he was the first to be subject to death. He was the first of all men upon the earth. His name means "first father" (Abraham 1:3).

Speaking of the existence of all spirits prior to their birth into mortality, the First Presidency of the Church in 1954, which included Joseph F. Smith, John R. Winter, and Anthon H. Lund, said: "All men and women are in the similitude of the universal Father and Mother, and are literally the sons and daughters of Deity"; as spirits they were the "offspring of celestial parentage" (*Man: His Origin and Destiny*, 351, 355). These spirit beings, the offspring of exalted parents, were men and women, appearing in all respects as mortal persons do, excepting only that their spirit bodies were made of a more pure and refined substance than the elements from which mortal bodies are made (Ether 3:16; Doctrine and Covenants 131:7–8).

The Lord has declared, "There is a law irrevocably decreed in heaven before the foundations of this world upon which all blessings are predicated—

"And when we obtain any blessing from God, it is by obedience to that law upon which it is predicated" (Doctrine and Covenants 130:20–21).

From eon to eon we prepared for our sojourn on this earth. We knew that we would be engaged in a battle for the souls of men, including our own, for there was war in our first estate and we knew that when Satan and his legions were cast out that the battle location would change but not the battle itself (Revelation 12; Doctrine and Covenants 76:25–49).

It is in this pre-earth estate that we find ten thousand times ten thousand evidences of the justice and goodness of God. We come to this earth knowing that we have been schooled and trained for whatever is asked of us here. There is great power within us. There are no surprises.

We also come clothed with power. We have the perfect assurance that victory will be ours. While we each may have Goliaths to face, we, like David, face them in the "name of the LORD of hosts, the God of the armies of Israel" (1 Samuel 17:45).

As we labor in the kingdom here we but resume associations formed long before our entrance into this our second estate. We hear the Master's voice for it is familiar to us. We respond by nature to truths with which we are familiar.

When we leave this life as disembodied spirits to gather to the paradise of God with family and loved ones to await the time of our resurrection, we will know those with whom we gather and they will know us. We will love them and rejoice in their company. We will no more be strangers to each other, memories of our past associations will envelope us, and we will commence to look after those from whom we have been separated with a deep love and concern.

While scores of scripture sustain the verity of that which has been said, the most eloquent evidence comes from the scripture of the heart. This is knowledge that we carry with us. It was born with us and is as natural to us as the light of the sun or the gentle breeze.

As we have the promise that our obedience to law and its attendant blessings will rise with us in the resurrection we then had the promise that all good works would follow us in birth into this life and bless us here. It can be no other way (Doctrine and Covenants 131:18–19). The handprint of God is easily seen on each commandment that he has given us.

Truth 25

The restored doctrine of a first estate, or premortal existence, opens the heavens to answer ten thousand questions for the honest truth seeker.

26

Is it God's doctrine to attack others?

"That which doth not edify is not of God, and is darkness" (Doctrine and Covenants 50:23). To edify is to lift or build. It has no kinship with that spirit which seeks to demean, to destroy, or to belittle.

A few years ago some missionaries of another faith called on our home and asked to share a message with us. I invited them in and seated them comfortably in our living room. I then went and gathered my family which I seated around them. I told them that we sought light and truth and if they had knowledge of God's plan for the salvation of his children that we did not have, we desired it. I further told them that if they had any such knowledge that we wanted it, that we would believe it, and that we would accept it. I committed my family there and then to being their disciples and to joining their Church. I told them that we would join with them in their missionary efforts.

That they might have some idea of what we then had, I briefly reviewed the story of the Restoration, including the restoration of the priesthood and the ordinances of salvation. I told them what a great blessing these things had been in our lives and how we had been blessed by them. I spoke specifically of eternal marriage and the continuation of the family unit.

I then invited them to share whatever they had that could add to the message we had received. They immediately began to attack all that I had said and tell us that we could have none of the things we professed. I interrupted them and reminded them that their invitation was to add to what we had, not seek to destroy it. Again, they began to attack all that I had said. Again, I interrupted them and reminded them of the invitation that I had given them. I invited them the third time to add to what we had and for the third time they commenced attacking what we had. I invited them to leave.

What seemed the most strange in all this was that having burned the house of my understanding to the ground they had no place for me to go. They had told me what I could not believe but said not a word about what I could believe.

Scores of times I have heard converts to the Church tell the story of their conversion, and scores of times I have heard how when they announced to their family that they were going to join the Church they were cast out by their family and disowned. I have often wondered why. Was it because they were going to renew their effort to live the Ten Commandments? Was it because they were going to take upon themselves the name of Christ in baptism and renew their efforts to live a Christlike life? Was it because they sought to honor their parents and be good citizens in the community? Was it because they had prayed and received an answer? Just what was the sin so grievous that they be eschewed by parents and disowned by family?

They carried no spirit that required that they belittle or attack that which they left. They simply sought to expand the light and truth their parents and family had given them. What spirit takes offense at that which is good? What spirit seeks to destroy rather than build?

Truth 26

All things are measured by their purpose. That which comes from God builds and edifies. That which comes from the prince of darkness demeans and destroys.

27

What happens to those who never hear the gospel preached?

The vast majority of people on earth today will live and die without having heard of the Bible, Christ, or God's plan for the salvation of his children. What of them? Every Latter-day Saint knows the answer. They will have the opportunity, before the Day of Judgment, to hear the gospel taught in a setting in which they are free to accept or reject it as they choose.

This doctrine stands unique to The Church of Jesus Christ of Latter-day Saints. Our declaration to all the world is that "the voice of the Lord is unto all men, and there is none to escape; and there is no eye that shall not see, neither ear that shall not hear, neither heart that shall not be penetrated" (Doctrine and Covenants 1:2).

While only Latter-day Saints embrace this doctrine it is clearly taught in the Bible. Consider the words of John:

> "The hour is coming, and now is, when the dead shall hear the voice of the Son of God: and they that hear shall live.
>
> "For as the Father hath life in himself; so hath he given to the Son to have life in himself;
>
> "And hath given him authority to execute judgment also, because he is the Son of man.
>
> "Marvel not at this: for the hour is coming, in the which all that are in the graves shall hear his voice,
>
> "And shall come forth; they that have done good, unto the resurrection of life; and they that have done evil, unto the resurrection of damnation" (John 5:25–29).

Peter taught the same principle in this language:

> "For Christ also hath once suffered for sins, the just for the unjust, that he might bring us to God, being put to death in the flesh but quickened by the Spirit:
>
> "By which also he went and preached unto the spirits in prison" (1Peter 3:18–19).

Many years before, Isaiah, speaking Messianically, had said: "The Spirit of the Lord God is upon me; because the LORD hath anointed me to preach good tidings unto the meek; he hath sent me to bind up the brokenhearted, to proclaim liberty to the captives, and the opening of the prison to them that are bound" (Isaiah 61:1–2).

While the historical Christian world refuses to see it, modern revelation affirms it. The single greatest revelation on this matter is Doctrine and Covenants 138, the vision of the redemption of the dead, which describes Christ's visit to the spirit world and the manner in which he organized his missionary forces to carry the gospel message to those who had not received it while in the flesh. Our temples, with their spires reaching to the heavens, stand as evidence of our faith in this principle.

We raise the question, "Why?" Not why the gospel is preached to those who did not, through no fault of their own, hear it while in the flesh, but why does historical Christianity go to such pains to deny it?

Who would not want it to be so? Who would not want family and loved ones to hear it? Who would not want them to be so blessed? Who would not want a God of justice and mercy? Who would not want God to have a plan for the salvation of all who desired it? Who would choose a God whose plan in the creation of the earth was to destroy or damn the greater part of his creation?

Could you in good conscience bear witnesses of such a God? Could you teach such a principle to a child?

Good doctrine sanctifies the soul (John 1:17). The Spirit cannot be constrained from declaring its goodness to the ends of the earth (Doctrine and Covenants 109:13).

> "Let the dead speak forth anthems of eternal praise to the King Immanuel, who hath ordained, before the world was, that which would enable us to redeem them out of their prison; for the prisoners shall go free.
>
> "Let the mountains shout for joy, and all ye valleys cry aloud; and all ye seas and dry lands tell the wonders of your Eternal King! And ye rivers, and brooks, and rills, flow down with gladness. Let the woods and all the trees of the field praise the Lord; and ye solid rocks weep for joy! And let the sun, moon, and the morning stars sing together, and let all the sons of God shout for joy! And let the eternal creations declare his name forever and ever! And again I say, how glorious is the voice we hear from heaven, proclaiming in our ears, glory, and salvation, and honor, and immortality, and eternal life; kingdoms, principalities, and powers!" (Doctrine and Covenants 128:22–23).

Truth 27

Either in this life or the next, all of God's creations will be granted the opportunity to receive all the blessings associated with the Kingdom of God.

28

Can one be neutral in the cause of Christ?

There are those who have left the Church but cannot leave it alone. For the most part they take refuge in Latter-day Saint families and communities. Thus they can include in their criticisms whatever annoys them at the moment for the benefit of any who will endure it patiently. If at some point they lost money in a business deal with a Latter-day Saint, it is because the Church taught the man how to cheat. If a good sister made a thoughtless remark it is because she was carefully trained to do so in Relief Society or sacrament meeting. If a neighbor offers help it is because they were assigned to do so, not because they have any real concern about the individual. Mormons do everything for statistics. Given that none of these statistics are ever shown to anyone, it is generally supposed they are given to Moroni who seals them up with the gold plates.

It appears that Latter-day Saints cannot do anything wrong on their own but need be taught how to do it in their church and quorum meetings.

I have now passed seventy years of age. I have always been active in the Church. If we suppose that from the time I was ten I began paying attention to what was being said, I have attended over 6,000 hours of instruction. I have spoken in over a thousand meetings, I have read hundreds of church books, I have taught full-time in church classrooms for over forty years, and spent countless hours interviewing and counseling members of the Church. In all of my experience I have never on a single occasion heard "the Church" or any member of it teach or suggest anyone ever do anything that was less than honorable. To blame the Church for the bad behavior of some of its members is like blaming a public school for a delinquent student.

When someone willfully chooses to break a commandment they are faced with the choice of repenting and making the matter right or proving the Church is false so they do not need to repent. This is the course these people have chosen. Having so chosen everything becomes bitter to their taste.

We make no claim to being a perfect people. There is not one of our number who has not made a mistake. Yet when you gather with the Saints you surround yourself with the best men and women on the earth.

The jackals but make the point. They are free to join what church they may. They generally do not do so. They just follow and nip and bark.

When I was the director of the Institute at the University of Washington, in Seattle, I was responsible for the in-service training of our early-morning seminary teachers. One of them shared this experience with me. He was driving from Seattle, to Salt Lake, to attend General Conference. Close to the Oregon border he was passed by a group of young people in a van that had been painted with an unusual array of bright colors. On its side was a sign which read "Former Mormons Who Have Been Saved!" The bait was set. They hoped to get some naive Mormons to pounce on.

As he continued his journey my friend saw where they had pulled off the road at an eating establishment. He said he was immediately overcome with hunger and pulled into the same place. He said it was easy to identify them from the noise they were making. He approached their table, and asked, "Are you the former Mormons who have been saved?" They were all too glad to identify themselves as such. He held up his hand to calm them down and said, "I just had one question that I wanted to ask. What commandment was it that you did not want to keep?"

The boisterous group was suddenly silent. It was as if they had been struck dumb. Not a word was spoken.

It is just as important to have the right enemies as it is to have the right friends. I have been to funerals and heard it said of the deceased that he or she never offended a soul, and I left wondering for what purpose the deceased had lived. If you live and die without your children knowing that there was a war going on for their souls I think you can have every assurance they and their children will not find themselves in the Church.

Truth 28

There is no neutrality where Christ and His gospel are concerned. You either stand with Christ or against him. Your soul belongs to he who you list to obey.

29

Angels: Who are they?

Angels have always been companions to the Lord and his people. They are and ever have been a sign of the true Church. Angels differ from mortals in that they are not bound by the laws that govern in our terrestrial world.

"And the office of their ministry is to call men unto repentance, and to fulfill and to do the work of the covenants of the Father, which he hath made unto the children of men, to prepare the way among the children of men, by declaring the word of Christ unto the chosen vessels of the Lord, that they may bear testimony of him" (Moroni 7:31).

There are five classes of angels:

1. Pre-earth spirits. Everyone who has been born into mortality was first a pre-earth spirit.

2. Disembodied spirits. Death is the separation of the body and the spirit. All who have passed from life to death have become disembodied spirits.

3. Translated beings. During the first 2,000 years of earth's

history—that is, from the Fall of Adam to the ministry of Melchizedek—it was not uncommon for faithful members of the Church to be translated. Since those times there have been occasional instances of translation, in which a special work of the ministry required the attributes of a physical body to accomplish. Translated beings function as missionaries and may even be called to labor on other planets. All translated beings must die in order to be resurrected (Doctrine and Covenants 133:53–55).

4. Resurrected beings. These are they who have experienced the inseparable union of the body and spirit never again to be divided. God and Christ are exalted, resurrected, and glorified men.

5. Evil spirits. In the scriptures we constantly read such phrases as, "the angel of the Lord," or "the angel of God," thus distinguishing them from the countless counterfeit angels that sought to deceive men.

There are twelve characteristics that will always be common to the true messenger or angel of the Lord.

1. They will hold the priesthood. "From Michael or Adam down to the present time, all [angels have declared] their dispensation, their rights, their keys, their honors, their majesty and glory, and the power of their priesthood; given line upon line, precept upon precept; here a little, and there a little; giving us consolation by holding for that which is to come, confirming our hope!" (Doctrine and Covenants 128:21).

2. "Angels speak by the power of the Holy Ghost" (2 Nephi 32:3).

3. Angels teach from scripture. (Joseph Smith—History 1:33–41)

4. Angels act on assignment. "The messenger who visited us on this occasion and conferred this Priesthood upon us, said that his name was John, the same that is called John the Baptist in the New Testament, and that he acted under the direction of Peter, James and John, who held the keys of the Priesthood of Melchizedek" (Joseph Smith—History 1:72).

5. All angels are people and have names: Michael, Gabriel, Raphael, John the Baptist, and Peter, James, and John are all examples.

6. Angels know us and address us by name. Of his first experience with the angel Moroni, Joseph Smith said, "He called me by name, and

said unto me that he was a messenger sent from the presence of God to me, and that his name was Moroni; that God had a work for me to do" (Joseph Smith—History 1:33).

7. In appearance angels look like their spirits (Doctrine and Covenants 77:2A).

8. The spirits of the just know our thoughts and feelings. Joseph Smith said, "The spirits of the just are exalted to a greater and more glorious work; hence they are blessed in their departure to the world of spirits. Enveloped in flaming fire, they are not far from us, and know and understand our thoughts, feelings, and motions, and are often pained therewith" (*Teachings of the Prophet Joseph Smith*, 326).

9. They attend our meetings, listen to our talks, hear us bear testimony, and often rejoice with us. The Lord has said, "Nevertheless, ye are blessed, for the testimony which ye have borne is recorded in heaven for the angels to look upon; and they rejoice over you, and your sins are forgiven you" (Doctrine and Covenants 62:3).

10. They read that which we have written with the same cause for concern and reasons to rejoice. Moroni freely quoted passages from the Old Testament that had not been included on the plates of brass. The Book of Mormon is described as "glad tidings for the dead; a voice of gladness for the living and the dead" (Doctrine and Covenants 128:19).

11. Angels will not do for us what we can do for ourselves.

12. True religion does not carry with it elements of fables or child's play. It does not consist of magic water, angels with wings, or of a god who is without body, parts, or passions. In its every particular, we find order and purpose. False messengers accost us regularly with accounts of their "out-of-body" experiences and the special message they have been commissioned to bring us. And what is that message? It is generally that we simply need to love one another. None of these accounts contain the suggestion that anyone needs to repent.

Truth 29

True messengers of God carry a message that is true. They always offend the adversary and those who are not keeping their covenants. This is service that all faithful Saints will be called upon to render.

30

What is a "living church"?

Suppose that I was a missionary for the historical Christian faith and you asked me the nature of my God. I could speak of a God of miracles, a God of prophets who spoke by way of revelation and prophecy and who took pen in hand and wrote volumes of scripture to preserve these sacred teachings. I could tell marvelous stories of healings and of the giving of special spiritual gifts to bless each member so that the congregation of the Saints could bless each other in turn.

Suppose I explained that God could not change his nature and continue to be God, and that he would be the same yesterday, today, and forever (Hebrews 13:8). In him there could not be so much as a shadow of changing, because for him to be less than I first described him would make him less than a God.

Then let us suppose the faith of the church changed—that having embraced the thinking of the Greek philosophers they had concluded that the original description of God was not adequate for our day and that God may not have really existed in earlier days either.

Both the Book of Mormon and the Doctrine and Covenants

restore the ancient promise that there will be signs that will follow them that believe. These signs include revelation, prophecy, healings, miracles, and all manner of gifts (Moroni 10:7–19; Doctrine and Covenants 46:6–33).

Every missionary who had the opportunity to grow up in the Church is a firsthand witness of these things and will be blessed by these same signs as they serve their mission. Though the God of the historical Christian church may have ceased to exist, the God of Mormonism is alive and well.

Experience common to Latter-day Saints includes the companionship of the Holy Ghost, father's blessings, patriarchal blessings, healings, dreams, scriptural insights, inspired utterances, and the granting of additional strength and knowledge.

To be a member of the only "true and living Church on the face of the whole earth" is a two-point proposition. To say that the Church is true is to say that it is founded on the laws and doctrines of heaven. It is to say that obedience to these laws will bring forth the blessings of heaven. To say that the Church is "living" is to say that its principles are simply black ink on white paper until they have been translated into action. Only by living a principle can we breathe the breath of life into it.

Truth 30
Among the characteristics by which true Latter-day Saints can always be identified are the gifts and blessings of heaven that attend them in their daily lives. Where these gifts are, miracles will be also.

31

Is "inerrancy" inerrant?

Hundreds of years ago the Roman Catholic Church clothed the Pope in the robes of inerrancy and infallibility. This meant that he was incapable of error in setting forth doctrine on faith and morals. This placed him in a position in which he could not be challenged. These positions came from various church councils.

Within the last two hundred years a large portion of the historical Christian world made a new application of this doctrine, one that had been unknown to every faithful soul from the days of Adam to that moment in time. The idea was that the scriptures were both "inerrant and infallible" as well. Declaring the Bible "inerrant" means that it is completely accurate and totally free from error. The idea associated with being "infallible" means that the preacher cannot communicate error while teaching from the Bible. He cannot make a mistake in his math, science, grammar, or anything else.

Perhaps it should be noted that there are no original manuscripts from which our Bible comes. No one can prove it inerrant. In any event, even if the assumption is true it is without purpose or value. As to the infallible preacher, his sermon ought to be added to the canon of scripture but cannot be because it is a fundamental tenant of those holding to this doctrine that the canon is sealed and nothing can be added to it. Discourses in this category are stored away with the original manuscripts of the Bible, which no living soul has ever seen or read.

In both instances this is simply a way to deny the Spirit of Revelation while trying to claim the Spirit of Revelation. A people to whom God speaks has no need for such bunglesome efforts. The purpose of this new doctrine is to give the Bible preacher the final word in all things just as it did the Pope. It eliminates the need to "ask of God," for all necessary questions have already been answered.

The chief argument in defense of the notion of inerrancy and infallibility is that if the Bible is wrong in one thing it could be wrong in all things. Were we to use this standard with our fellow men, there would not be a man upon the earth that could trust another.

The reader may be helped by reviewing basic principles about the Bible. One need not be a Bible scholar to know that in the history of religion most believers lived before the existence of the Bible. The Bible that we have today was unknown to those who lived at the time of Christ. There is not now and never has been agreement on what books belong in the Bible. There is a Jewish Bible, a Catholic Bible, and a Protestant Bible.

There is not a single instance where the New Testament quotes from the Old Testament in the same language used in the Old Testament. Christ preached in Aramaic, the New Testament is recorded in Greek, and we quote him in English.

The men who wrote the Bible had no Bible at the time they wrote. We are continually getting new translations of the Bible, which are believed by many to be an improvement over the translations of the past. The Church created the Bible, the Bible didn't create the Church. The various books chosen for each Bible embrace a telling of the story that favors the translator's doctrinal interests. In fact, there are more variations among Bible manuscripts than there are words in the New Testament.

Truth 31

Inerrancy and infallibility are earmarks of false religion. The gospel of Jesus Christ requires that the true saint will, in the process of living the truth, grow from grace to grace until they come to a fullness of truth.

32

Can common ground be sacred ground?

The single greatest heresy in missionary work is the idea that we seek common ground with those we teach. Any time a missionary tells an investigator that we share common ground he or she has testified against the need for the Restoration. Joseph and Hyrum Smith did not die in Carthage Jail to assure that we could believe in the same things everyone else already believed.

There are well over twenty thousand different Christian denominations. When I have asked how I am to find a sure path amid such confusion I have always been told that though various Christian churches disagreed on matters of lesser importance they were all united on the basic and important doctrines— here they shared common ground. This response raises at least two important questions: First, what are the lesser or optional commandments that Christ gave? And second, what principles of the gospel are negotiable? Furthermore, one might ask if there are really principles upon which all the thousands of denominations agree.

It is not enough for these churches to say, "Well, we all believe in the Bible." The question is, what in the Bible do they believe? Do they all believe in the necessity of baptism? And if not, are they all united in the rejection of this ordinance God required of His Only Begotten Son? Yet another question steps forward which also demands an answer. What if their common ground unites them on principles that are false? For instance, what if they all ascribe to the creeds of men? This forces on us certain beliefs that cannot be sustained by the Bible. In like manner, what of the doctrine of the Holy Trinity or the idea that the heavens are sealed, that all revelation that God intended man to have has been given and nothing can be added to it?

If these things are numbered among the common-ground doctrines, then how are we to know it? We have no acceptable scriptural text to sustain them and we have robbed God of a voice whereby he can reject them.

In a revelation given to those of our day for the purpose of responding to the kind of difficulties just noted, the Lord said:

> "But ye are commanded in all things to ask of God, who giveth liberally; and that which the Spirit testifies unto you even so I would that ye should do in all holiness of heart, walking uprightly before me, considering the end of your salvation, doing all things with prayer and thanksgiving, that ye may not be seduced by evil spirits, or doctrines of devils, or the commandments of men; for some are of men, and others of devils" (Doctrine and Covenants 46:7).

If ever there was a doctrine born to confusion and mischief it is the doctrine of common ground. Where the truths of salvation are concerned there is no neutrality. The Lord told his missionaries, "Ye are not sent forth to be taught, but to teach the children of men the things which I have put unto your hands by the power of my Spirit;

"And ye are to be taught from on high. Sanctify yourselves and ye shall be endowed with power, that ye may give even as I have spoken" (Doctrine and Covenants 43:15–16).

Truth 32

Our divine directive is to be in the world but not of it. The greatest heresy in missionary work is the concept that we want to be just like everyone else. We do not answer questions about our faith by making it appear that we are just like others. Ours is not common ground, it is sacred ground. It is where the heavens open and the God of heaven speaks.

Do Mormons wear magic underwear?

Members of The Church of Jesus Christ of Latter-day Saints who have been endowed in the temple wear what is called a garment. The garment is a modest form of underclothing which, for us, carries religious significance. The Greek meaning for the word garment is "to be clothed."

In an attempt to embarrass Latter-day Saints it has become increasingly common for people to ask about our "magic underwear." One would think the embarrassment would be on the part of the person asking such a private question rather than the person being questioned. I know of no other equal discourtesy in the form of questions asked of people of other faiths.

The truth of the matter is that not only is the person asking the question making a show of their rudeness but of their Biblical ignorance. The imagery of garments and the metaphor of changing clothing to enhance one's power is the most often used teaching device in the Bible.

The story begins in Eden after God has married Adam and Eve and taught them the law of sacrifice. We have 4,000 years of history suggesting to us that the animal being sacrificed was a lamb. It was from the skin of a lamb that the garment given to them was made.

"Unto Adam also and to his wife did the LORD God make coats of skins, and clothed them" (Genesis 3:21). Here, the word "skins" could also have been translated as garments or tunics.

So before Adam and Eve left their "father and mother" (Genesis 2:24) to go out into the world they were clothed in coats of skins that stood as a constant reminder to them that in and through the blood of the Lamb they would be protected from all the effects of the Fall. The coats of skins in which Adam and Eve were clothed stood as a constant reminder that through the blood of the Lamb they would be protected from all the evils of this world.

When one recognizes that the story of Adam and Eve was intended as a universal story, that in the Eden story Adam and Eve are types and shadows of all God's children, and that their story is our story, this story and all that follows in the Bible becomes very meaningful and personal.

People of faith do not equate a blessing of protection with magic. For instance, Paul's direction that we "put on the whole armor of God" is not the kind of thing that we would tease our neighbors about trying to do (Ephesians 6:11).

If we leave the setting of the Old Testament and turn to the New Testament we can find the resurrected Savior instructing the Twelve to "tarry ye in the city of Jerusalem, until ye be endued with power from on high" (Luke 24:49). The footnote for "endued" in our Latter-day Saint Bible reads "or clothed." When the promise was given to the Twelve that they would be clothed in power from on high, no one could have accused them of supposing the were to go into all the world and practice magic.

As there are some that are not true to their marital vows, so there are some who are not true to other promises and covenants they have made with the Lord. Warning against such Christ said, "Beware of false prophets, which come to you in sheep's clothing, but inwardly they are ravening wolves" (Matthew 7:15). The reference to "sheep's clothing" was understood quite literally and refers to the same clothing with which Adam and Eve where clothed in Eden.

As to the matter of holding the priesthood and declaring the gospel, the Apostle Paul declared that, "No man taketh this honour unto himself, but he that is called of God, as was Aaron" (Hebrews 5:5).

If we go back to the Old Testament to see how Aaron was called, we learn he and all who labored in the priesthood were first to be washed, anointed, clothed in their priesthood robes, and consecrated before Israel (Exodus 40:12–15).

In the Book of Zechariah we read the story of a high priest by the name of Joshua. The story is a temple council scene in which Satan challenges Joshua's right to his high priestly office because he could not prove himself a direct descendent of Aaron. He had been born in captivity and so the assumption was that his mother had been raped.

> "And the LORD said unto Satan, The LORD rebuke thee, O Satan, even the LORD that hath chosen Jerusalem rebuke thee: is not this a brand plucked out of the fire?
>
> "Now Joshua was clothed with filthy garments, and stood before the angel.
>
> "And he answered and spake unto those that stood before him, saying, Take away the filthy garments from him. And unto him he said, Behold, I have caused thine iniquity to pass from thee, and I will clothe thee with change of raiment.
>
> "And I said, Let them set a fair mitre upon his head. So they set a fair mitre upon his head, and clothed him with garments. And the angel of the LORD stood by.
>
> "And the angel of the LORD protested unto Joshua, saying,
>
> "Thus saith the LORD of hosts; If thou wilt walk in my ways, and if thou will keep my charge, then thou shalt also judge my house, and shalt also keep my courts, and I will give thee place to walk among these [those in the heavenly council] that stand by" (Zechariah 3:2–7).

In the Book of Moses we have an interesting story in which the Lord directs Enoch to the top of a mountain. "And it came to pass that I turned and went up on the mount; and as I stood upon the mount, I beheld the heavens open, and I was clothed upon with glory" (Moses 7:3).

We return to the New Testament to consider the parable of the wedding feast. The Savior tells the story: The King [of heaven] sent out his servants to announce the marriage of his [Only Begotten] son. As was the custom of the day, the King would provide the robe in which everyone was to be dressed. All were to be clothed in white robes that were alike in appearance. That the King supplied the robe was a reminder of his grace, which is the same for all, and that everyone was to be clothed in righteousness. However, a man came to the feast clothed in filthy garments. As was the tradition, the wedding was held at night. The palace was lighted by the glory of the King, who had the man in the filthy garment bound and then cast outside to outer darkness (Matthew 22:11–14).

The more familiar one is with the Bible, the more familiar one is with such stories. Similarly, the more familiar one is with mocking the faith of others, the more familiar one is with the spirit of the adversary.

Truth 33
Sacred clothing has always been a part of true religion.

34

Can true religion ask for less than our best?

It does not take money to pay tithing—it takes faith. "Faith, then, is the first great governing principle which has power, dominion, and authority over all things; by it they exist, by it they are upheld, by it they are changed, or by it they remain, agreeable to the will of God. Without it there is no power, and without power there could be neither creation nor existence!" (Lectures on Faith 1:24).

All churches would like to have their members pay tithing, but they do not do so because their members do not have the faith to pay it. In like manner, they would like to be able to send out missionaries like ours but they cannot. They simply do not have the faith among their numbers to get that many young men and young women with the faith to accept a call to serve at their own expense wherever they might be sent to serve for the required time. Other churches would like to introduce our family home evening program and our visiting teaching and home teaching programs along with a host of other programs, but they do not because they simply do not have the faith to make them work.

The key to salvation is not in believing in Christ but in following him. It is found in doing, not professing. "Let us here observe," suggested the Prophet Joseph Smith, "that a religion that does not require the sacrifice of all things never has power sufficient to produce the faith necessary unto life and salvation. For, from the first existence of man, the faith necessary unto the enjoyment of life and salvation never could be obtained without the sacrifice of all earthly things. It was through this sacrifice, and this only, that God has ordained that men should enjoy eternal life; and it is through the medium of the sacrifice of all earthly things that men do actually know that they are doing the things that are well pleasing in the sight of God. When a man has offered in sacrifice all that he has for the truth's sake, not even withholding his life, and believing before God that he has been called to make this sacrifice because he seeks to do His will, he does know, most assuredly, that God does and will accept his sacrifice and offering and that he has not, nor will not seek His face in vain. Under these circumstances, then, he can obtain the faith necessary for him to lay hold on eternal life" (Lectures on Faith 6:7).

Faith unto salvation comes from doing, not simply believing. Only in the world of religion will you find people that believe that ordinances performed for you despite lack of faith or obedience will bless you.

Truth 34

True worship consists of believing as God believes, thinking as God thinks, and doing as God would do. It consists of countless things we do to bless others, and it refines our souls in the process.

35

Why does the cause of truth always attract scoundrels?

Before the development of the printing press there were no two books on the face of earth that were the same. Most books took the form of a collection of scrolls. All were handwritten texts, and there was no way to make a serious comparison of the variant manuscripts.

Jude counseled the saints to "earnestly contend for the faith which was once delivered unto the saints" (Jude 1:3). Modern commentaries interpret this to mean to be true to the Bible as it was delivered to you. The idea being conveyed is that somehow the Bible just appeared and the faithful should stand in its defense. A more thoughtful reading of the text suggests that reference is being made to the gospel as taught in the Old Testament rather to a compilation of books that would not be gathered together for hundreds of years. The places cited are Egypt, Sodom, and Gomorrah. The characters are Cain, Balaam, and Korah, and the chief writer was Enoch, who was kept from a place in the canon until the days of Joseph Smith.

Jude's warning continues: "For there are certain men crept in unawares, who were before of old ordained to this condemnation, ungodly men, turning the grace of our God into lasciviousness, and denying the only Lord God, and Lord Jesus Christ" (Jude 1:4).

The book that was formed over the course of thousands of years was not just given to Jude and those in his ward like a lesson plan on a given Sunday morning. The Bible went through the hands of many scribes, and some of them were wicked men who freely changed the text as it served their purpose. How can you say "We are wise, and we have the law of the Lord" when scribes with their lying pens have falsified the text containing the law? To the scribes of his day the Savior said: "Woe unto you, lawyers! For ye have taken away the key of knowledge: ye entered not in yourselves, and them that were entering in ye hindered" (Luke 11:52).

The Joseph Smith Translation renders it thus, "Woe unto you, lawyers! For ye have taken away the key of knowledge, the fullness of the scriptures; ye enter not in yourselves into the kingdom; and those who were entering in, ye hindered" (Joseph Smith Translation, Luke 11:52).

Every Primary graduate knows that we believe in the Bible as far as it is translated correctly. This does not suggest that translators today are somehow ignorant of mistakes in translation that have been and are presently being made. We are a bright people and are as capable of translating ancient records as any people on earth.

The great matter and the heart of our message does not center in translation but transmission. Our concern is with the plain and precious things that have been taken from it. They have been restored to us by the score in the Book of Mormon as well as in the Pearl of Great Price and the Doctrine and Covenants.

If the Bible had not been tampered with in significant ways we would not need the Book of Mormon. No commentary will ever be written that sustains the Bible with power and prophecy the way the Book of Mormon does. There are no anti-Book of Mormon arguments that are not at the same time anti-Bible arguments. There are no anti-Joseph Smith arguments that are not at the same time anti-Jesus Christ arguments.

Truth 35

Every gospel doctrine is greeted by the adversary with a counter doctrine. All gospel principles and practices have their counterfeit. The only church whose doctrines and practices have remained unchanged from dispensation to dispensation was restored to us by the Prophet Joseph Smith. Ours is not a new religion but a restoration of the faith of the ancients.

36
How many baptisms can there be?

Perhaps no gospel subject better illustrates the doctrinal confusion in the historical Christian world than the ordinance of baptism. The role of John the Baptist was so important that it was prophesied from Old Testament times (Malachi 3:1).

In the Gospel of John the temple priests sent a delegation down to Bethabara, where John had baptized Jesus and a great many others. Their purpose was to find out which of the promised prophets John claimed to be. To their first question he said that he was not the Christ. In response to their second question he said that he was not Elias (meaning Elijah). In response to their third question he confessed that he was the prophet spoken of by Isaiah, who referred to him as "the voice of him that crieth in the wilderness, Prepare ye the way of the Lord, make straight in the desert a highway for our God" (Isaiah 40:3). The Book of Mormon gives even more detailed descriptions of these events (1 Nephi 10:7–10; 11:27).

Jesus walked from Galilee to Jordan, a distance of several days, to be baptized. When he approached his cousin, the man holding the keys of the Aaronic Priesthood and the authority over the ordinance of baptism, the Baptist originally refused him. Christ reminded John that it was necessary that he do so "to fufil all righteousness" (Matthew 3:15). This means that for the two of them to be justified—that is, approved by the law of God—John needed to baptize Jesus. John's ministry was "to overthrow the kingdom of the Jews, and to make straight the way of the Lord before the face of his people, to prepare them for the coming of the Lord, whose hand is given all power" (Doctrine and Covenants 84:28).

Christ in the Malachi prophecy of these events was given the name "messenger of the covenant" (Malachi 3:1). The gospel of Jesus Christ is the covenant, and baptism is the gate by which one enters the kingdom of God (2 Nephi 31:17). In 2 Nephi 31, Nephi gives five reasons why Christ was baptized:

1. Christ was baptized as a witness of his humility before the Father.
2. Christ was baptized to show that he would be obedient in keeping all the commandments of the Father.
3. Christ was baptized so that he might work out his own salvation.
4. Christ was baptized so that he might be an example in all things.
5. Christ was baptized so that he might enjoy the companionship of the Holy Ghost.

Christ was baptized in obedience to the commandment of the Father. In ancient and modern times Christ charged the Apostles to go into all the world telling everyone that they must be baptized or be damned.

Those in the evangelic world tell us that baptism is not necessary. Those in the Catholic world baptize infants by sprinkling, even though these children are too young to sin, repent, so much as say the word "God," or retain any memory of the event. Latter-day Saints hold that all must be baptized, as was the Savior, by immersion and by authority that traces itself to John the Baptist, and that such a baptism is necessary for one to be saved in the kingdom of God. Latter-day Saints believe the age of accountability for baptism is eight years and that all those who did not have the opportunity to be baptized in this life will have that opportunity extended to them in the world of disembodied spirits prior to the resurrection. Those choosing to be baptized, having had the gospel preached to them, can comply with the commandment by proxy baptism performed in a temple built for that purpose.

> ## Truth 36
> The authority to perform a valid baptism is certainly evidence that the Church is true. Such authority can be found only with those who were baptized as were Jesus and John.

37

Is tampering with the Bible alive and well?

The most popular passage in the Bible is John 3:16. You have heard it quoted so often that you have memorized it unknowingly. Singularly, it constitutes a perfect example of how the true meaning of the Bible has been distorted by translators and theologians, creating a god and gospel of their own making.

In Nephi's vision of the creation of America, the nation that was destined to restore religious freedom to the world, the Prophet described a people coming out from religious captivity in Europe to America, where they were delivered by the power of God out of the hands of all other people. He also beheld a book which they brought with them (1 Nephi 13:1–20). That book was the Geneva Bible, the edition of the Bible that these religious Pilgrims brought with them as their guide in the building of America. The Geneva Bible was the work of Reformers exiled to Europe at a time when the Catholic church and various kings kept all but clergy and Latin scholars from reading scripture. In England it became a capital crime to read or quote publicly from the Bible in the English language.

In the Geneva Bible, John 3:16 reads as follows: "For God so loveth the world, that he hath given his only begotten Son, that whosoever believeth in him, should not perish, but have everlasting life."

The King James Version of the Bible came in answer to the marginal readings in the Geneva Bible, primarily as they attacked the idea of the divine right of kings. It took more than 150 years for this version to gain general acceptance. It was the King James Version that Joseph Smith was reading that led him into the Sacred Grove. As rendered in the King James Version used by Latter-day Saints today, John 3:16 reads, "For God so loved the world that he gave his only begotten Son, that whosoever believeth in him should not perish, but have everlasting life."

Then the great change came. In modern translations, such as the New International Version or the Revised Standard Version, you would be hard-pressed to find such a rendering to the verse. The text is translated so that it reads, God so loved the world that he gave his "only Son" or his "one and only Son" that we should not perish. The word begotten is omitted.

The idea that Christ is the begotten Son of God does not square with the creeds of men. It clearly implies that God is an actual being, that he is in reality a father, and that Jesus of Nazareth is actually his Son.

At the same time that it robs God of his personhood, his fatherhood, and Christ of his rightful place as the child born of God to Mary, it destroys the plan of salvation. No longer do we have a Son who inherited the power of life from his immortal father, or a Son who also had the power to lay down his life and take it up again. This omission thus destroys the doctrine of the Atonement and the resurrection.

This subtle change in text robs all of us of the claim to being the spirit sons and daughters of God and of the attendant hope of resurrection. Thus this text captures how the creeds of men have taken so much of life and meaning out of the Bible and have thereby dramatized the reality of a universal apostasy and the need for a restoration of all things.

Truth 37

John 3:16, the bible's most popular verse, has often been changed from "God's only begotten Son" to "God's only Son," thus denying Christ's divine Sonship and our rightful place as sons and daughters of God. Joseph Smith has both preserved and restored this concept.

38

Are Mormons secretive?

Mormons, we are told, are a secretive people, doing things in their temples from which the general public is excluded. The criticism, ironically, is generally given by those who complain that we are annoying because our missionaries and members are forever seeking the opportunity to share our message with them and then seeking to get our new converts to go to the temple.

Before our temples are dedicated we hold an open house and invite all who would like to tour the temple and learn about its place and purpose in our system of worship. Tens of thousands of people attend these open houses.

Perhaps what is taking place here can be best illustrated in a parable. Suppose there is a great university that teaches a graduate class in extended family relationships. All who meet the requirements for graduate study are encouraged to attend. The class has an honor code with which all who attend are expected to conform. It includes the wearing of academic robes while attending the class. What you get out of the class will be dependent on the preparation you have made for it. You can attend the class as often as you desire. The university, however, is constantly criticized by those who have chosen not to meet the requirements to attend the class—and who would not have chosen to take the class in any case.

The Lord has always commanded his people to gather to holy ground. For instance, Moses and the house of Israel were commanded to go to Mount Sinai. Previously, Moses had been commanded to remove his shoes on the side of the Holy Mount "for the place whereon [he stood was] holy ground" (Exodus 3:5).

The purpose for gathering to holy places is to make covenants and receive instruction in things not to be known to the world (Exodus 19). Prior to doing so members must sanctify themselves, for no unclean thing can enter the presence of the Lord. The promise given with regard to temples in our dispensation is as follows: "And verily I say unto you, let this house be built in my name, that I may reveal mine ordinances therein unto my people;

"For I deign to reveal unto my church things which have been kept hid from before the foundation of the world, things that pertain to the dispensation of the fulness of times" (Doctrine and Covenants 124:40–41).

These are not promises reserved for the leaders of the Church but rather promises given to all members who will prepare themselves to go to the temple. All have the right to know the sacred things of the kingdom with the admonition that they cast not their "pearls before swine" (Matthew 7:6).

It is in our restored temple worship that we find those sacred truths that God has commissioned us to share with all the world. This is yet another sure sign of the true church.

As Moses was commanded to take off his shoes to stand upon holy ground, so we have been commanded to teach these truths, but only in holy places.

Truth 38

There are no secrets in Mormonism. All are invited to see, hear, and know for themselves.

Who's in charge?

The churches of men are governed by the policies and practices of men. They are the creations of men, and it is each church's right to govern that which it has created. The Church of Jesus Christ of Latter-day Saints is the Lord's church, however, and he runs it. The Ten Commandments are not the work of a committee, nor were the children of Israel called upon to ratify them. Matthew stated the principle concisely: "Every plant, which my heavenly Father hath not planted, shall be rooted up" (Matthew 15:13).

Ours is a God who speaks. From the days of Adam to the ends of the earth, this is the divinely ordered system: "And thus the Gospel began to be preached, from the beginning, being declared by holy angels sent forth from the presence of God, and by his own voice, and by the gift of the Holy Ghost.

"And thus all things were confirmed unto Adam, by an holy ordinance, and the Gospel preached, and a decree sent forth, that it should be in the world, until the end thereof; and thus it was. Amen" (Moses 5:58–59).

We refer to revelation given to the leaders of the Church for the purpose of directing the Church as institutional revelation. Such revelation always comes through proper priesthood channels. We refer to revelation given to an individual for personal direction as personal revelation.

In recent times it has become the practice of those who are spiritually unstable to seek to give direction to our priesthood leaders which reinforces their own biases. In so doing they are breaking the covenant they made to sustain their priesthood leaders and cutting themselves off from the light given to direct the Church. They also forfeit the right to personal revelation.

It is to those we sustain as prophets, seers, and revelators that we turn for light. We sustain each of these men as apostles. As it comes to us from the Greek, the word *apostle* means "one sent forth" (*apo*, "forth," and *stello*, "to send"). Inherent in the word *apostle* is the idea of a commission and the further thought of authorization. Of themselves the Apostles have no authority and espouse no doctrines. The divinely sent teachers profess authority only in the name of Christ and only on his errand.

The idea is captured perfectly in the Book of Mormon as it speaks of the role of the Twelve called during Christ's visit to the Nephites, "And when they had ministered those same words which Jesus had spoken—nothing varying from the words which Jesus had spoken—behold, they knelt again and prayed to the Father in the name of Jesus" (3 Nephi 19:8).

Elder Bruce R. McConkie explained the principle in this manner:

"I often think as I go around the Church and preach in various meetings that it just does not make a snap of the fingers difference to me what I am talking about. I do not care what I talk about. All I am concerned with is getting in tune with the Spirit and expressing the thoughts, in the best language and way that I can, that are implanted by the power of the Spirit. The Lord knows what a congregation needs to hear, and he has provided a means to give that revelation to every preacher and every teacher" (Bruce R. McConkie in *A Man Raised Up: The*

Teachings of Bruce R. McConkie, ed. David F. Boone, 85).

We do not create the doctrines of the gospel. We faithfully deliver the message we have been given. Far too often people come to our priesthood and auxiliary classes with questions designed to reinforce what they want to hear rather than to find the mind and will of God.

The claim can be made to being the only true and living Church only if we are acting as the Lord's agents rather than as the spokesperson for someone else. If it is the Lord's church he will run it. The message will be his. We have no right to either add to or take from the gospel as it has been revealed to us (3 Nephi 11:40). As the Lord has said, "My thoughts are not your thoughts, neither are your ways my ways, saith the LORD. For as the heavens are higher than the earth, so are my ways higher than your ways, and my thoughts than your thoughts" (Isaiah 55:8–9).

Truth 39

The Church by necessity and design will always be at odds with the world. If we do not clearly stand independent of the world it can only be because we are of the world.

Eve: Temptress or prophetess?

Satan insults and fights that which he finds the most threatening. If something threatens him, that thing must be evidence that the Church is true. This principle applies perfectly to the role of woman as she has been cast from the time of the Fall. Historical Christianity has painted Eve as the architect of all the world's woes. The Restored gospel completely reverses such an idea, placing Eve in a place of honor second only to Mary, the mother of Christ. As with Eve, so it is with all women, for each woman in her own right is Eve.

From the revelations of the Restoration we learn that woman is the spirit daughter of divine parents, a God in embryo, a being created in his image and likeness, the eternal companion with man, and the crown jewel of the creation.

While there are some women who have convinced themselves that the Church has in some way demeaned them, they will be unable to find any other theology that so exalts and honors them. We sometimes hear it argued that women are not considered the equals of men because they do not hold the priesthood. This argument leaves much wanting. To argue that if something is not the same as something else, that it is not equal, is at best, shallow.

Gospel eqality is found in oneness. Only a woman can conceive and give birth to a child but she can't do it without the aid of a man. Similarly, the fullness of all gospel blessings are a shared fullness between a man and a woman. One star does not shine brighter than the other. The shared glory granted to both men and women in the Restored gospel seems a perfect evidence of the truthfulness of the Church.

Truth 40
Through the restored church, Father Adam and Mother Eve are returned to their exalted position over all humankind, thus unlocking the purpose of the three pillars of eternity: the Creation, the Fall and the Atonement.

Why is the Atonement central to all truth?

All gospel principles find life and purpose in the Atonement. A correct understanding of the Atonement (at-one-ment) requires a knowledge of the Fall and of the Divine Sonship of Christ. Without a sound understanding of these two principles no legitimate claim can be made to having possession of the plan of salvation.

One's knowledge must be sure and certain where these principles are concerned. The three pillars of eternity are the Creation, the Fall, and the Atonement. None can be understood in isolation of the others. Without a proper understanding of the Creation there can be no meaningful understanding of the Fall, and without a meaningful understanding of the Fall there can be no meaningful understanding of the reconciliation brought by Christ to restore us to our pre-Fall state and reconcile us with the Father. Such an understanding requires the knowledge that God is indeed our Eternal Father, separate and distinct from the other members of the Godhead. It also requires the knowledge that we are literally the Father's spirit children; that Christ is literally his son in the flesh; that Mary is literally his mother (from whom Jesus inherited blood, or the ability to die); that God, who is an exalted and resurrected man, does not have the capacity to die; and that it was a blood Fall that required a blood Atonement.

An understanding of these principles is found only in The Church of Jesus Christ of Latter-day Saints, but for the most part, Latter-day Saints seem to have an inadequate understanding of this principle. When we hear a talk on the Atonement in one of our meetings it is almost always confined to the fact that because of the Atonement of Christ we can receive a remission of sins. Our understanding needs to extend to embrace the understanding that the Atonement "sustains, supports, and gives life and force to all other gospel doctrines. It is the foundation upon which all truth rests, and all things grow out of it and come because of it" (McConkie, Bruce R., *Mormon Doctrine*, 60).

Because of Christ's Atonement we can repent of our sins and be made clean; be baptized and receive the gift of the Holy Ghost; receive the blessings of the priesthood, including the temple endowment and eternal marriage; be made perfect and come forth in the morning of the first resurrection to inherit all things, and ultimately, become as God is.

Christ died to preserve the truth. Had there been no Atonement there would be no truth and we would all have become devils, servants of that devil who first sought to dispose of God in the grand council of heaven.

Truth 41

Were it not for the Atonement of Christ, there would be no plan of salvation. The Atonement breathes life into all the principles and ordinances of the gospel.

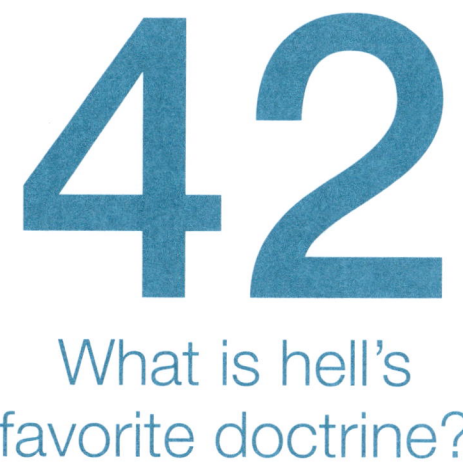

What is hell's favorite doctrine?

Given that the principles of the gospel are everlastingly the same, the arguments against those principles remain the same also. Standing opposite the principle of continuous revelation, for instance, is the doctrine of sufficiency. The doctrine of sufficiency holds that what has been given in the past is sufficient, and thus the heavens are sealed to additional light and knowledge. One arguing for this doctrine would likely say, "My father plowed fields with the aid of a horse, read by the light of a candle and had no indoor plumbing. It was good enough for those who lived generations before, and it is good enough for us today."

In the Joseph Smith Translation we have a wonderful account of the Savior teaching the Twelve how to handle this issue. It begins with his injunction to the Twelve to challenge their investigators to ask of God with the attendant promise that those who ask, knock, and seek will receive divine guidance as they need it. The disciples who had been doing this reported that those they sought to teach would respond by saying:

"We have the law [meaning the Law of Moses] for our salvation, and that is sufficient for us.

"Then Jesus answered, and said unto the disciples, thus shall ye say unto them,

"What man among you, having a son, and he shall be standing out, and shall say, Father, open thy house that I may come in and sup with thee, will not say, Come in, my son; for mine is thine, and thine is mine?" (Joseph Smith Translation, Matthew 7:12–17).

The analogy is clear: no father would say to his younger son, "I taught your brother to speak and that is sufficient—I will not teach you to speak. I taught him a trade, I fed him, and I clothed him. Surely that is sufficient, and I will do no more."

The very idea is contrary to fatherhood and to the nature of God. Truth is not in competition with itself. All truth is made stronger in its association with other truths. To give your son or daughter a truth is but to prepare them to receive another. The Old Testament does not weaken one's understanding of the New Testament. The purpose of the Book of Mormon is to sustain and enhance our understanding of the Bible. Anyone who truly believes the Bible will believe the Book of Mormon. One simply cannot say that he believes what Jesus said on one day of the week but not on the others. One cannot say, "I believe what he preached in the Old World, but not what he preached in the New World," or "I believe what he said to the Nephites but not what he said to the other tribes of Israel when he visited and taught them."

Ours is not a hearsay religion. It is not a record of the acts of a loving Father in ancient times that tired of teaching his children and decided to become a stern and fearful teacher instead of a loving father. No single book of the Bible was written to be understood through the prism of the creeds of men. As originally written, it all stood independent of the world's stranglehold.

In New Testament times, all Christians called upon the Father in the name of Christ. The Fatherhood of Christ was the crowning doctrine of the New Testament. Every exchange that existed between the Christ and the Most High God was an exchange between a loving Father and a beloved Son. This constitutes the key that unlocks the universe and gives meaning to all other doctrines, including, as we have seen, the Atonement.

To deny the need for continuous revelation to give life and meaning to current revelation is to deny the light of the sun to the spring planting. It is to reduce revelation to black ink on white paper. When the God of heaven chooses to erase those principles he personally espoused or to invite their re-reading through creeds written by councils of men, you may know of a surety that you no longer have possession of the gospel of Jesus Christ.

Truth 42
Hell's favorite doctrine is that the heavens are sealed and that God has no need to speak to us in our day.

43

Do spiritual gifts exist today?

The Apostle Paul tells us that in the meridian dispensation, members of the Church were identified by the possession of special spiritual gifts. These gifts, coupled with the Holy Ghost, gave the Saints spiritual talents that enabled them to do things to strengthen their fellow Saints in countless different ways (1 Corinthians 12). The idea is something akin to a large family in which each member has a special gift which enables them to either protect or bless the family.

During the long period of apostate darkness we are told that those gifts would be lost and that men would lose both the power of God and the gift of the Holy Ghost. The powers of heaven were to be rejected in preference to the wisdom of men. Nephi described what would take place in this manner, "Cursed is he that putteth his trust in man, or maketh flesh his arm, or shall hearken unto the precepts of men, save their precepts shall be given by the power of the Holy Ghost" (2 Nephi 28:31).

Significantly, the last chapter in the Book of Mormon promises the restoration of spiritual gifts (Moroni 10:8-19), as does Doctrine and Covenants 46.

Spiritual gifts are as distinct and unique as fingerprints. No two people have been gifted in the same way. The gifts come after baptism, when the Holy Ghost endows you with a particular capacity that places you in a position to bless your ward, stake and family in a manner that no one else can (Doctrine and Covenants 46:10–13).

All those so endowed by the Holy Ghost are to share their gifts in a like manner. This means that there is no one in the Church who cannot make a unique and distinct contribution to edify and strengthen others in the Church. At the same time it means that there is no one in the Church that cannot be blessed by the special gift you have been given.

There is no better evidence that a church is true than the fact that the Holy Ghost is actively manifesting himself through its members. A church which God will not attend has little to suggest it as the only true and living church. Spiritual gifts are a sure sign of the true church.

Truth 43

There is no better evidence that the Church is true than the fact that the fruits of the Holy Ghost are manifest in the lives of its members.

Does knowing require doing?

Some years ago I developed an interest in running. I shared my interest with a fellow faculty member whose office was right next to mine. He was the best-read person I ever met on the subject of running. My commitments were such that I had little time to read much about the subject, but I did get out and run regularly. To my knowledge, my friend never ran a step in his life. I ran, he read. One month I ran a couple of marathons, and that month he read a couple more books. Which one of us, do you think, knew the most about running?

If we liken this illustration to knowing about God, we ask who knows the most about him, the vocal proponent or the disciple who acts as he would act, believes as he believes, and does as he would do? Is the knowledge that saves academic or experiential? Experience suggests to us that if you want to be a baseball player you play baseball in preference to reading books on the subject. I know of no instance when a baseball team met and the coach handed out copies of a book and then sent the team home to meet again on game day.

I do not mean to suggest that there is no advantage to be gained by thoughtful scripture study; however, such study takes on appreciably greater value when sustained with a concerted effort to make the principles being taught in the scriptures an active part of your life.

We have spoken before of those in the religious world who assume themselves saved because of the vigor with which they witness of Christ. Their boldness often gets lost in rudeness and they are quick to condemn any who dare to disagree with them. We have also noted those whose salvation rests in ritual and the authority of priesthood leaders. We return to that discussion to establish what holy writ is telling us.

It will be remembered that in his great intercessory prayer offered at the Last Supper, Christ said, "This is life eternal, that they [his disciples] might know thee the only true God, and Jesus Christ, whom [Heavenly Father had] sent" (John 17:3). Though the term is used with various shades of meaning, "to know God" in the purest scriptural sense is to have an intimate or covenant relationship with him.

The Old Testament refers both to knowing God, and to a man knowing his wife, meaning conceiving a child with her. Both phrases use the same Hebrew word, *yada*. As a man was to leave father and mother and cleave unto this wife and thus become one flesh with her, so he was to leave the things of the world and cleave unto his God and become one with him. As faithfulness in marriage was essential to the nurturing of love, so faithfulness in keeping gospel covenants was understood to be necessary in obtaining knowledge of God. As love for one's spouse is strengthened in sacrifice and devotion, so the knowledge of God is obtained in living one's covenants with exactness and honor.

Similarly, we read in the New Testament that Joseph did not know Mary until after the birth of Christ (Matthew 1:25); as we just noted, it is life eternal to know God and Jesus Christ. Both verses use the same Greek word, *ginosko*.

Among the children of Israel, knowledge was not reducible to an act of intellect that apprehended an object. The true meaning was in a recognition of the one who, through his creations, was already there. To know was to be disposed to obey. Thus to know God is to be like God. A wicked man cannot know God, even though he may be able to quote every passage of scripture ever penned. A righteous man knows

God, but only to the extent of his righteousness.

We see this priniciple illustrated throughout the scriptures:

- "But he that doeth truth cometh to the light, that his deeds may be made manifest, that they are wrought in God" (John 3:21).
- "If we say that we have fellowship with him, and walk in darkness, we lie, and do not the truth" (1 John 1:6).
- "He that saith, I know him, and keepeth not his commandments, is a liar, and the truth is not in him" (1 John 2:4).
- "And he that repents not, from him shall be taken even the light which he has received; for my Spirit shall not always strive with man, saith the Lord of Hosts" (Doctrine and Covenants 1:33).

It has often been observed that the Lord could devise a more effective way to do missionary work than to send out teenage missionaries. If that were true, the Lord would do it. The making of a missionary is the working of a miracle, and it works in the same way on senior missionaries as it does on young men and women, if the senior missionaries will work as hard and be as obedient as their junior counterparts.

There is no better evidence of the truthfulness of the gospel than the way it changes the lives of both the missionaries and those they teach. That those who accept the gospel have their lives changed by it is axiomatic. That it changes the lives of the missionaries so that in the process of missionary work they work out their own salvation is one of the distinctive revelations of the Restoration, one which no other Church on the face of the earth can match. It is a great, sustaining witness that the message they bear is true.

Truth 44

The reading of scripture alone does not change lives, but living the principles found in the scriptures does. It is for this reason that we are a lay church and are constantly called upon to serve.

45

Are men and women equal in the Church?

There are women within the Church who seem quite convinced that they have been demeaned because they have not been given the priesthood or been called to hold a high office or position. Salvation, however, is not an office; spirituality is not an office. Courage, grace, and faith are not offices either.

We can survive armed mobs and even armies, what we cannot survive are ignorant mothers. It would rather seem that strength grows out of obedience, not priesthood office held. It seems a little ironic to seek the blessings that come only through obedience by disobedience. The idea reminds me of a young man I once knew who, when asked why he had chosen to drop out of school to join the Marines, said, "Because I was sick and tired of having people tell me what to do."

There is no office on the face of the earth that requires a more complete surrender of personal will than that of an Apostle. If a woman is seeking such rights of expression or to have her views heard, she could not be more at odds with her objective than in seeking the priesthood.

Let the reader be reminded that it is the Lord's Church and he runs it. Members of the Church have no say and never did have any say in the formulation of its doctrines. If the Church of Jesus Christ allows anyone other than Christ a say of any sort in the formation of its doctrines, it ceases at that moment to be the Church of Christ. There is little difference between praying for a change in a particular doctrine or praying for God to surrender his role to you.

Doctrines come by revelation; they are eternal and do not change. Procedures are man-made and can be modified or dispensed with. Any seeking to modify the doctrines of the Church have placed themselves in competition with God and are at the bidding of the adversary.

Truth 45

The restored gospel exalts womanhood. The fullness of gospel blessings are only available as a man and woman stand side by side as equal partners.

46
Who can speak in the name of the Lord?

No one by birth or by choice has the right to speak in the name of the President of the United States or the governor of the state in which they reside. Such offices as president or governor must be properly conferred upon you. In like manner, no one has the right to act for and in behalf of God without being called. If God wants a particular person to act in his name, he must both call him or her and also announce that call to all the world.

It will not do to have the required revelation be personal—that is, God cannot tell me that I am to rule over you. If the Lord did want me to rule over you, he would tell us both. Were it to be otherwise, what we would have in the name of churches would be nothing more than competition. Religion would be reduced to a swarm of competing businesses all marketing Jesus.

This is what the scriptures call priestcraft, of which the Lord said: "He commandeth that there shall be no priestcrafts; for, behold, priestcrafts are that men preach and set themselves up for a light unto the world, that they may get gain and praise of the world; but they seek not the welfare of Zion" (2 Nephi 26:29).

In a related warning we are told: "Wherefore, let all men beware how they take my name in their lips—

"For behold, verily I say, that many there be who are under this condemnation, who use the name of the Lord, and use it in vain, having not authority" (Doctrine and Covenants 63:61–62).

In the Church and kingdom of God there will be no paid ministry. There will be no competing for offices or positions. There will be calls made for people to serve for a time and season, and there will be releases given after an appropriate period of service. People will be asked to serve in capacities that they would rather not, and to sacrifice their time and talents. In the true Church, this will be the expected norm. You do not choose the congregation that you meet with nor the time of the meetings. You simply serve as you are called to serve.

Truth 46

To preach the gospel in the name of Christ without being properly called to do so is to take the Lord's name in vain.

What is the plan of happiness?

Lehi, in one of the finest expressions of the plan of salvation ever given, said, "Adam fell that men might be; and men are, that they might have joy" (2 Nephi 2:25). This is to say that the earth was created for men (meaning humankind) and that Adam partook of the forbidden fruit so that Eve could find fulfillment as a woman in motherhood, and that in the family unit, they as parents could find meaning and purpose in life.

Mother Eve proved herself equally articulate when she said: "Were it not for our transgression we never should have had seed, and never should have known good and evil, and the joy of our redemption, and the eternal life which God giveth unto all the obedient" (Moses 5:11).

Interestingly, the word "plan" is not found in the Bible. However, phrases like "plan of redemption" and "plan of happiness" are found thirty-one times in the revelations of the Restoration.

A Messianic prophecy that foretold the words Christ would use to introduce his earthly ministry reads as follows: "The Spirit of the Lord

GOD is upon me; because the Lord hath anointed me to preach good tidings unto the meek; he hath sent me to bind up the brokenhearted, to proclaim liberty to the captives, and the opening of the prison to them that are bound" (Isaiah 61:1).

The captives or prisoners to whom reference is made are those in the world of disembodied spirits who did not have the opportunity to accept the gospel in this life (Doctrine and Covenants 128:22-25; 138:31-35). Teaching this principle Joseph Smith said, "And now, my dearly beloved brethren and sisters, let me assure you that these are principles in relation to the dead and the living that cannot be lightly passed over, as pertaining to our salvation. For their salvation is necessary and essential to our salvation, as Paul says concerning the fathers—that they without us cannot be made perfect—neither can we without our dead be made perfect. . . .

"For it is necessary in the ushering in of the dispensation of the fulness of times, which dispensation is now beginning to usher in, that a whole and complete and perfect union, and welding together of dispensations, and keys, and powers, and glories should take place, and be revealed from the days of Adam even to the present time" (Doctrine and Covenants 128:15,18).

This is the plan of happiness. The plan calls for creation and eternal preservation of the family unit. This plan will always be sustained by principles of righteousness, persuasion, long-suffering, gentleness and meekness, and love unfeigned (Doctrine and 121:36, 41). By contrast, that which comes from the prince of darkness will exercise control, dominion, or compulsion over the souls of men in unrighteousness (Doctrine and Covenants 121:37).

Truth 47

The plan of salvation is not in flux. God is "the same yesterday, today, and forever" (Doctrine and Covenants 20:12). Perfect faith could not be exercised in any other being. Latter-day Saints alone lay claim to such a God.

48

Why did God create and people the earth?

All scripture is not of equal worth; all ordinances are not of equal importance. For example, baptism is more important than blessing a child, and receiving the gift of the Holy Ghost is more important than being set apart for an office or position. We have ordinances of blessing and ordinances of salvation. The most important single thing that any member of this Church does in this life is to marry the right person, in the right place, by the right authority.

The composite of all saving ordinances is known as the new and everlasting covenant. The same phrase is used to describe eternal marriage because all other ordinances lead to it. The earth was created so that a man and a woman could be married (Doctrine and Covenants 49:16–17).

This is certainly one of the most distinctive doctrines of the Restoration. It is ironically one of the most often criticized and often borrowed of our doctrines. It is a doctrine of the heart and simply bears witness of itself.

Time is one of the great measures of our commitment to that which is eternal. If a young man came to a young woman and said "I love you two months' worth," she probably wouldn't have much interest in his proposal unless her interest in him was as limited as his interest in her. Years ago when I was in the military, a young lady to whom I was a home teacher married a fellow outside the Church. Their plan was to get around to eternal marriage later. Unfortunately, he fell asleep while driving on their honeymoon and had his life taken. Some months later she married again, and again her newly wedded spouse fell asleep while driving and lost his life. There is a degree of judgment and sense that those getting married must bring to the altar with them.

On one occasion I stood for hours in an evacuation hospital on the battlefields of Vietnam while skilled surgeons sought to save a young soldier's life. The last thing he said to me before he underwent anesthesia was, "I wish I had married my wife in the temple."

It is for us to choose what we take with us into the life to come, but our choices are limited. We take our character, what we believe (and what we do not believe), we take our faith, and we take the composite of what we have become. We take the promises of the covenants that have been made to us if we have kept those promises, and we take the curses of covenants unkept. We take what we are and nothing else.

We take with us the love we have for our spouse and children. This love will continue to grow in the hereafter as it has here. It is our greatest treasure, and like all treasures, it must be guarded and protected. To have failed to marry in the temple is to have joined with far too many who were too busy to do as God asked and instead placed their own agendas in precedence to the plan of happiness.

We offer no more perfect evidence of the purpose, goodness, and truthfulness of the gospel of Jesus Christ than the new and everlasting covenant.

Truth 48

No other principle gives more meaning and purpose to life than marriage. Nothing could be further from the mind of God than to have a man and woman love and serve each other for the course of a lifetime only to take this sacred relationship from them in death.

49

What becomes of those who die as children?

There is not a single sentence in either the Old or New Testaments that gives answer to the question as to what becomes of the child who dies without arriving at the age of accountability. All such children leave this life without having ever had the ability to accept or reject Christ. This absence of commentary is a perfect illustration that plain and precious things have been taken from the sacred writ and that the plan of salvation does not and cannot rest with those who cannot give an adequate answer to such a question.

The principles involved were first revealed in the Book of Mormon. Mormon received a revelation on the matter in which he was told that Christ came into the world to call sinners, not those who are whole, to repentance. The curse of Adam does not rest on little children because Satan has no power over those who are incapable of sin. Thus God declared that it is "solemn mockery" to baptize little children (Moroni 8:8–9). He continues, "And their little children need no repentance, neither baptism. Behold, baptism is unto repentance to the fulfilling the commandments unto the remission of sins.

"But little children are alive in Christ, even from the foundation of the world; if not so, God is a partial God, and also a changeable God, and a respecter to persons; for how many little children have died with baptism!" (Moroni 8:11–12).

Joseph Smith taught, "The Lord takes many away even in infancy, that they may escape the envy of man, and the sorrows and evils of this present world; they were too pure, too lovely, to live on earth; therefore if rightly considered, instead of mourning we have reason to rejoice as they are delivered from evil, and we shall soon have them again" (*Teachings of the Prophet Joseph Smith*, 196–197).

The principle here involved presents a perfect expression of justice. Those who will be blessed to receive the gospel in the spirit world must comply with the same principles as they would have complied with in the flesh. They must, in the language of Peter, "be judged according to men in the flesh" (Peter 4:6). From the vision of the celestial kingdom we learn that in order for such individuals to be saved, they must die without having had the opportunity to accept the gospel in this life, God must judge that if they had the opportunity come to them they would have acted on it, and God must also judge that they would have done so with all their hearts (Doctrine and Covenants 137:7–9).

To this the Prophet added, "All children who die before they arrive at the years of accountability are saved in the celestial kingdom of heaven" (Doctrine 137:10). As it is with temporal life, so it is with the life that follows: not everyone wants to be paid what they are worth. Only a just man wants to receive justice. When people make gods unto themselves it is because they do not want the alternative.

Truth 49

A God who, with the aid of loving parents, creates a child without the interest and power to save that child, is no god at all.

50
The veil of stupidity!

Joseph Smith spoke of a "veil of stupidity" that covers the minds of men (*Teachings of the Prophet Joseph Smith*, 13). This veil is brought on by disobedience, or refusal to stand in the light, and results in the shabbiest thinking which is reserved for principles that are eternal.

It always seemed a strange thing to me that people reserved their worst thinking for religion. A glance at an obituary often makes this point. There we read announcements about the blessings that are to be enjoyed by the deceased which are generally at complete odds with the theology of the church in which they professed membership. It is of particular interest that no punishment for failure to keep any standard or commandment is to be read. Obituaries simply do not carry such things. Here the family gets to sit in judgment on its members.

A God, we read, who they believed is not a personal being, and who is described in their chosen creed as without body, parts, or passions, will embrace them. They will join with loved ones in a family unit—one that their faith denies—and look down on and bless loved ones throughout all future times of trial. Somehow, these people are able to lay claim to all of this without ascribing to any particular standard, making God and the gospel simply a scare tactic but not something that you would take very seriously.

The most popular commentary on what is taking place here was given to us by Lehi. He explained how many would argue that there is no law and hence no sin, and because there is no sin there will be no punishment (2 Nephi 2:13). Simply stated, the sequence of events is to convince oneself that there is no law and hence no sin, and because there is no sin there is no such thing as righteousness or wickedness, and since one cannot be rid of sin one cannot find happiness either. This places the professor of such a faith in a position to pick and choose what they want to believe in and what they do not. Oscar W. McConkie, my grandfather, stated the matter well: "I never indulged in the deceitful hope that I could win God's favor while I, at the same time, opposed him in any particular." It is not a small God with puny ideas and negotiable standards that we worship.

Truth 50

It is hypocritical for someone to say they have studied the history of the Church and found in it too many inconsistencies to believe that the Church is true. The history of the Church is simply an account of things that happened to those who were members of the Church, and if those people died true to the faith, then that is their testimony and that is our history. Do you see it? For those who lived it there were no inconsistencies. Joseph and Hyrum sealed their testimony of the Book of Mormon and the revelations of the Restoration with their blood in Carthage Jail. You cannot use their history as an excuse to be anything less than faithful. As to what we call history, they lived it; whatever the flaws were, they knew them—they knew them a thousand times better than we ever will—and they died in the faith. They did not waver, they did not doubt, and they did not fail. When the time came they mounted their horses and rode to Carthage. That was their testimony. That is our history.

For other works from this author, including *Valiant in the Testimony of Christ*, *Between the Lines* and *Christ, Covenants and Salvation* in electronic and paperback form, please visit **www.mcconkiebooks.com**

For bulk purchases, or general questions, please email:
info@mcconkiebooks.com